The Illustrations of William Makepeace

THACKERAY

The Illustrations of William Makepeace
THACKERAY

JOHN BUCHANAN-BROWN

David and Charles
Newton Abbot London North Pomfret (Vt)

FOR MY WIFE

British Library Cataloguing in Publication Data

Buchanan-Brown, John
The Illustrations of William Makepeace Thackeray.
1. Thackeray, William Makepeace   2. Illustration
of books — England
I. Title   II. Thackeray, William Makepeace
741'.092'4   NC978.5.T/

ISBN 0-7135-7811-2

© John Buchanan-Brown 1979

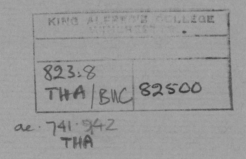
Typeset by ABM Typographics Limited
and printed in Great Britain
by Biddles Limited, Guildford
for David & Charles (Publishers) Limited
Brunel House   Newton Abbot   Devon

Published in the United States of America
by David & Charles Inc
North Pomfret   Vermont 05053   USA

Contents

Preface

The title defines the scope of this book: namely, what might be called Thackeray's public art—the published illustrations which he executed, principally for his own writings. It excludes, except as a point of reference, what might be termed his private art, the innumerable watercolours, drawings and pen-sketches which he made for his own amusement and that of his family and friends and to decorate his correspondence.

Although, then, this study is restricted to one aspect of this great man's achievement, it will not, I trust, be judged *constricted* on this account. Although his drawings cannot be set on the same high plane as the books they illustrate, they suffer unfairly from the very excellence of the writing. And, while Thackeray became the novelist rather than the painter he had hoped to be, and hence his illustrations came to be executed for his own books exclusively and not for those of others, it needs to be emphasized that he worked *as an artist in his own right* on the *Punch* of Leech and Doyle. No study of English nineteenth-century book illustration can afford to neglect Thackeray as a practitioner, particularly when the books which he illustrated are among the masterpieces of nineteenth-century English literature.

Thackeray was not only a practising artist but a respected critic of contemporary art. Since this study is concerned with his rôle as illustrator, I have concentrated upon the attitudes expressed in his essays and reviews towards book illustration and generally ignored those towards painting at large. However, I feel in a measure absolved from this task by the meticulous analysis which Professor John Carey has already made, in *Thackeray the Prodigal Genius*, of this art criticism, and his application of it to expand our understanding and enjoyment of Thackeray as a writer.

For obvious reasons, I have not attempted a detailed account of Thackeray's life, rather confining my attentions to those aspects of it which are strictly relevant to his development as an artist. General information is based upon Professor Gordon N. Ray's biography of the novelist (two volumes: 1955–8) and matters of detail upon his edition of Thackeray's letters and private papers.

Finally, I would like to express my thanks to Thackeray's literary heiress, Mrs Belinda Norman-Butler, for permission to reprint copyright material from *The Letters and Private Papers of W. M. Thackeray* (edited by Gordon N. Ray: Harvard University Press and Oxford University Press: four volumes: 1945–6) and to reproduce two illustrations from *A Thackeray Alphabet* (John Murray: 1929).

London
January 1979

Introduction

On Tuesday evening, 22 December 1863, William Makepeace Thackeray dined at the Garrick Club and on the following day was unwell and confined to bed. There seemed to be no cause for alarm. At about midnight, the novelist's mother, who slept in the next room, heard the sounds of retching: when they came to wake him on the Thursday morning, they found that Thackeray had died of apoplexy during the night. Among the tributes to the man and the writer which this sudden and shocking death evoked, perhaps the most moving is the essay of his intimate friend, the Edinburgh doctor and man of letters, John Brown. 'On the death of Thackeray' opens with what might serve as the writer's epitaph:

> Mr Thackeray was so much greater, so much nobler than his works, great and noble as they are, that it is difficult to speak of him without apparent excess. What a loss to the world the disappearance of that large, acute, and fine understanding; that searching inevitable inner and outer eye; that keen and yet kindly satiric touch; that wonderful humour and play of soul!... This, with his truthfulness, his scorn of exaggeration in thought or word, and his deep, wide, loving sympathy for the entire round of human wants and miseries, goes far to make his works in the best, because in a practical sense, wholesome, moral, honest, and 'of good report'.

Despite the circumstances, despite the fact that this is written about a friend of his later years who had enjoyed the same close personal intimacy as did his university friend Edward Fitzgerald in Thackeray's youth and early manhood, it is a judgement with which those who can meet Thackeray only in his writings, and particularly in his *Letters and Private Papers*, will concur.

1 The Formative Years

Such were the moral and intellectual qualities developed during a life in which he had made himself an exceedingly popular lecturer on both sides of the Atlantic, a literary editor of the highest calibre of the phenomenally successful *Cornhill Magazine*, a notable magazine-writer—and one of England's very greatest novelists. This solid achievement was, in its turn, based upon an inherent ability, for both his grandfather and his father had made their mark in the very different sphere of the Honourable East India Company's service. Thackeray's grandfather, William Makepeace (1749–1813), had been an able and none too scrupulous official of the eighteenth-century mould who had made his fortune; the novelist's father, Richmond (1781–1815), had risen swiftly and spectacularly to the important post of Assistant Secretary to the Board of Revenue in Calcutta and would clearly have been destined for still greater things had he not died at the early age of thirty-four. The novelist must have inherited something of the energies of both. Then, too, the father was a man of some culture, in whom flowered that literary and intellectual strain which had produced a Provost of King's College, Cambridge, in the Thackeray family tree.

Yet, however much these hereditary qualities may have influenced the later development of the novelist, Thackeray in his early twenties showed little or no sign of possessing any of them. On the contrary; after a reasonably respectable school career at Charterhouse, he went up to Trinity College, Cambridge, in 1829, only to leave a year later without taking a degree and with nothing to show for his academic year but debts. Among them was the considerable sum of £1500 lost to sharpers at the gaming-table, for Thackeray had acquired the compulsion to gamble. He was to lose considerably more over the next three years in the hells of London and Paris and Germany. Indeed, he had begun to visit the Continent while still an undergraduate, spending vacations in Paris in 1829 and 1830, and it was to the Continent that he went on leaving Cambridge in the summer of 1830, spending some six months in the congenial atmosphere of Weimar.

He next had thoughts of the Bar, being admitted to the Inner Temple on 3 June 1831. However, a year's desultory reading convinced him that he was unsuited to the grind of legal business and, after a further stay in Paris, he started an abortive bill-discounting business at the beginning of 1833. This did not last long: in May 1833 he purchased part-ownership of a weekly, *The National Standard*.

It was in some sense a logical step for the undergraduate journalist (part-founder of *The Snob* and its successor, *The Gownsman*) who had already begun in 1831 to contribute reviews to *Fraser's Magazine*. It was probable that his purchase of *The National Standard* stemmed directly from his connexion with *Fraser's*.

His diary for 16 April 1832 records a meeting with the magazine's editor, the brilliant but ramshackle Irish journalist, William Maginn. On 2 May he notes that 'Dr Maginn called & took me to the Standard shewing me the mysteries of printing & writing leading articles'. Ten days later the young man was 'introduced to Fraser of F's Magazine.—Thought him neither clever or good very different from hearty witty Maginn, who is a very loveable man I think.' Clearly Maginn, who was editor and co-founder with James Fraser of *Fraser's Magazine*, had laid himself out to be pleasant to young Thackeray, who was as ripe for plucking by the literary as he had been by the card sharpers.

The upshot was a very welcome loan of £500 to the impecunious Maginn and the purchase of a partnership in *The National Standard*, a transaction which Thackeray was in later life to regret, if his disparaging references in *Lovel the Widower* to the greenhorn who purchased the literary magazine *The Museum* are autobiographical. In any event, Thackeray appears to have had no more idea of using his newly purchased position than as the means to enjoy the Bohemian life of the Parisian artist by appointing himself the paper's Paris correspondent and departing for the Continent in June 1833.

That Thackeray at twenty-two should have been no more than the wealthy young literary and artistic *flâneur*, living above the income from the money made by his father in India and wasting the capital on ill-advised literary speculations and in the gambling dens of London and Paris, can be attributed to his Anglo-Indian background. Like all English children he had to be sent home at the age of five, reaching England on 15 June 1817. He was brought up by his maternal grandmother, Mrs Becher, at Fareham in Hampshire. As with so many other Anglo-Indian children, the pangs of separation and the exile from the princely trappings of Calcutta to the middle-class atmosphere of Fareham were made all the more bitter by the horrors of a bad private school, in Southampton. But this ordeal, if such it can be called, was short. Two years later he moved to a good school in Chiswick and in the same year his mother, who had re-married with her first love, Captain Carmichael-Smyth, returned to England. In 1822 when Thackeray entered Charterhouse, Carmichael-Smyth was given his majority and appointed Governor of Addiscombe, the East India Company's military academy in Surrey, a post which he held for two years until his retirement to Ottery St Mary, in Devon. Their house, Larkbeare, became the family home for the remainder of Thackeray's schooldays and for his brief university career.

Larkbeare is, of course, the Fairoaks of *Pendennis;* and, while it is dangerous to read too much into that admittedly autobiographical novel, Helen Pendennis is a portrait of Mrs Carmichael-Smyth, just as the Colonel in the later *The Newcomes* is based upon her husband. Their respective fictional treatments of Pen and Clive only too probably reflect the indulgence with which Anglo–Indian parents tried to compensate the child for its loss of their loving care and to win back the trust and affection which they may subconsciously have felt that they had forfeited. Add to this that the Carmichael-Smyth's marriage was childless and it is hardly surprising that the young Thackeray should show so many symptoms of the spoiled child, in his gambling and his extravagance, and in his playing with journalism and art, for, as Thackeray was to recall many years later in a letter to his mother, 'at twenty you know we all thought I was a genius at drawing'. With the hindsight of 1862 he added: 'O the mistakes that people make about themselves!'

Yet the mistake was only natural when the optimism of a twenty-year-old and the admiration of a doting family exaggerated the degree of an undoubted talent, a talent which had been exhibited from an early age. The very first letter which Thackeray wrote to his mother soon after his arrival in England on 3 July 1817, shortly before his sixth birthday, is decorated with the recognizable sketch of a man on horseback while, in a postscript, his great-aunt Ann Becher adds: 'William drew me your house in Calcutta not omitting his monkey looking out of the window & Black Betty at the top drying her Towells.'

This talent for impromtu sketching, demonstrated in adult life on page after page of his letters, with its uncanny knack of catching an immediate likeness, was developed during his schooldays when the ability to caricature authority became a source of notoriety and of popularity. A copy of Rollin's *Ancient History*, extra illustrated, survives from this period,[1] and undoubtedly the incident of 'Young Raphael' (plate 126) described in *Doctor Birch and his young Friends* is based upon personal experience. His letters to his mother reveal that he spent a disproportionate amount of his time as an undergraduate in sketching, and it is while at Cambridge that he experimented with steel etching (plate 10).[2]

During a vacation in Paris he not only studied the prints in the Bibliothèque du Roi, but told his mother (in a letter of 28 July 1829) that 'I subscribe to a circulating drawing Library where I may have plenty of things to copy for 6frs a month'. During his eight months in Germany in 1830–1, after he left Cambridge, and especially during his stay in Weimar, his sketchbook was much in use not only to record the scenery (in fact he found the spectacular rather palled during his leisurely journey down the Rhine) but as a social adjunct. His sketches, and particularly those which he made for their children, were remembered by his hosts at the little German court many years later.

However, at this stage Thackeray appears to have had little artistic training and it was only when he was established in Paris as the correspondent of his paper *The National Standard* that he began seriously to study art, writing to his mother at the end of October 1833 that 'I spend all day now dear Mother at [Le Poittevin's] Atelier & am very well satisfied with the progress wh: I make, I think that in a year were I to work hard I might paint something worth looking at'.

This idyllic existence was, however, beginning to draw to an end. Although Thackeray was steadily dissipating his inheritance—mainly through his compulsive gambling[3] but also through extravagant living, his unsuccessful bill-discounting venture, the loan to William Maginn and the purchase of *The National Standard*—nevertheless, some £11,000 remained of the original £20,000 which his father had left in trust for him. But then at the end of 1833, came the stunning news of the failure of the Calcutta bank with which these funds were deposited. At a stroke Thackeray's income was reduced to a bare £100 per annum from his few remaining investments—not that this seems to have changed his attitude to life very much.

The National Standard staggered on, but was clearly ailing: the last number appeared on 1 February 1834. With this failure of his journalistic hopes, Thackeray seems to have determined to develop his artistic talents, settling in Paris in the autumn of that year as an art student. On 5 October he wrote to his mother that he had 'been working very hard at the Louvre, & begin tomorrow at the Life Academy, wh: has not yet been open: I have had no time to make original drawings, & I think it is as well I should not for some time to come'. Three days later, in a letter to Edward Fitzgerald, he elaborates: 'I have copied at the Louvre two Titian portraits Leonardo's Charles VII Interior by de Hoog, & women playing on the harpsicholls by Terburg—They are all of them very bad, but I don't despair—tonight I begin at the life academy.'

And Thackeray enjoyed the *vie de Bohème;* as he remarked in the essay 'On the French School of Painting, in his *Paris Sketch Book:*

> The life of the young artist here is the easiest, merriest, dirtiest existence possible . . . he arrives at his atelier at a tolerably early hour and labours among a score of companions as poor as himself. Each gentleman has his favourite tobacco-pipe; and the pictures are painted in the midst of a cloud of smoke and a din of puns and choice French slang, and a roar of choruses, of which no one can form an idea who has not been present at such an assembly. . . . In this company . . . the French student of arts passes his days and acquires knowledge; how he passes his evenings, at what theatres, at what *guinguettes*, in company with what seducing little milliner, there is no need to say.

Unfortunately Thackeray himself felt that he had made little progress in his studies and, writing to his painter friend Frank Stone on 17 April 1833, he was forced to confess:

> As for myself—I am in a state of despair . . . and have lately become so disgusted with myself and art and everything belonging to it, that for a month past I have been lying on a sofa reading novels, and never touching a pencil. In these six months I have not done a thing worth looking at.

Probably because of his dissatisfaction, Thackeray turned again to journalism (he had begun in 1834 once more to contribute reviews to *Fraser's Magazine*) by angling for the post of Constantinople correspondent for *The Morning Chronicle*. To this end he approached John Payne Collier, a fellow-member of the Garrick Club and long connected with the paper, to sponsor his application. The move came to nothing, but in the meantime life in Paris was most agreeable, with the Latin Quarter, the theatres, the galleries (particularly the Louvre) and the British colony—the cheap living in France being the main attraction for middle-class British families and, in particular, for retired officers and officials of the East India Company living on their pensions. It was a society to which Thackeray had, as it were, hereditary right of entry; moreover, his aunt, Charlotte Ritchie, and her husband had been members of it since their move to Paris five years before. (Thackeray had always been on very close terms with this family. When they had lived in London, theirs had been a home from home to the Charterhouse schoolboy, to whom they had acted almost as second parents.) It was in this social circle that the crucial event of Thackeray's life occurred, when he met and fell in love with Isabella Shawe.

Isabella's mother, a colonel's widow, has been immortalized in the story 'Denis Haggerty's Wife' and as 'The Campaigner' in *The Newcomes*, but Thackeray's closest portrait of this poisonous woman—she must have been mentally unbalanced—is that of Mrs Baynes in *Philip*, where Philip Firmin's courtship of Charlotte Baynes mirrors Thackeray's wooing of Isabella Shawe. Like the hero of his novel, when Thackeray finally married Isabella, on

20 August 1836, it was in the teeth of the opposition of his mother-in-law, who had employed every means at her disposal, fair and foul, to break the engagement of her daughter to this penniless young man. That she finally gave her reluctant consent was due only to his appointment as Paris correspondent of *The Constitutional*.

This was a radical newspaper founded in 1836 with Samuel Laman Blanchard as editor; Thackeray's friend Charles Buller was a leader-writer for it. Thackeray's step-father, Major Carmichael-Smyth, was a substantial shareholder and appointed one of the directors, although he forewent any remuneration to secure the Paris appointment for his stepson. The salary of between £300 and £400 a year from the paper was the financial basis of the Thackeray household, and very fragile it was to prove. Perhaps because it was too bourgeois for the working-class radical and too radical for the middle-class liberal, *The Constitutional* ran for barely a year, the last number appearing on 1 July 1837, a month after the birth of the Thackeray's eldest child, Anne.

Now began the ten-year struggle to establish himself as a writer which was to be the making of Thackeray as a man and as a novelist. However, more immediate was the pressing problem of finance. Help from his stepfather was out of the question: the failure of *The Constitutional* had so seriously embarrassed him that the Carmichael-Smyths removed from London to Paris to economize (less kindly, it was hinted that the Major had fled in order to avoid his creditors). Although other relations rallied to their support, clearly the young family had to secure some sort of income, however precarious, and Thackeray accordingly moved them to London where he could market his two available talents, his literary and artistic abilities.

In both fields he had some slight achievement; although he had made his literary début as reviewer and journalist, he might well have considered that, despite some failures, art held more promise than writing.

True that the fifteen sketches reproduced as woodcuts in *The National Standard* between May and August 1833 are mere trifles,[4] but a more considerable talent—and it is an artistic rather than a literary talent—is evidenced in the first book which Thackeray published in 1836, under the pseudonym of Théophile Wagstaffe.

Flore et Zéphyr comprised nine lithographic plates satirizing the ballet, of which Thackeray was a lifelong devotee, the great ballerina Marie Taglioni, whose art he admired deeply, and the celebrated male dancer, Perrot. In Paris Thackeray had developed an appreciation for the satiric litho-print, and his own efforts were now transferred to the stone by Edward Morton (see plates 13–16). There is also evidence that in the early 1830s he executed a number of individual portraits and squibs in this medium for the London printsellers.[5]

Meanwhile, his skill with the etcher's needle must have shown some improvement on his undergraduate efforts and, before the collapse of *The Constitutional*, he had made abortive efforts in this line of illustration for French and British publishers. For example, he mentions in a letter to his mother from Paris of 23 July 1835 that

> I have at this moment a good offer a publisher here will give me a good deal to do— for I have been highly recommended to him, but he wants views of cities wh: are out of my line. I have made five drawings of one place here in Paris, and have cut them up one after another for they were too bad to show him, these repeated disappointments make me ready to hang myself, in fact I am as disheartened as a man need be—for I can do nothing—and yet I have got the stuff to make as good a painter as the best of them.

Then, on 7 October 1836, he writes to Fitzgerald:

> I had a very handsome commission of £50 to make some etchings, but I have tried and made such miserable work that I must give them up I find. It is a sad disappointment, for I had hoped to have done much in that line.

Even more interestingly, we find him writing to William Harrison Ainsworth in January 1837:

Dear Ainsworth, I'll do anything that's possible to heighten the charms of your immortal book the admirable Crichton; and with this noble purpose this little scrap I write on, to say I'll do you drawings such as never man had sight on; and neat vignettes wh: all the world will surely take delight on; . . .

Soon afterwards he wrote to Ainsworth's publisher, John Macrone, promising to 'send you half a dozen drawings by Wednesday's Post . . . I tried them on the Copper, but what I did was so bad, that I felt mortified at my failure, and did not care to write to you about it'; he goes on to correct the impression that 'I had finished all the drawings . . . three finished & a parcel of Sketches'. This candid admission of failure as an etcher—and perhaps of the poor quality of the drawings—decided Macrone against commissioning Thackeray. Ainsworth's novel had to wait another twelve years for an illustrated edition, and this time the artist responsible was the celebrated Phiz (Hablot Knight Browne).

A further disappointment was the rejection of his application to illustrate *Pickwick Papers* when, in 1837, Seymour's suicide and Buss' manifest incompetence had imperilled the continuation of the serial. Here again Phiz was to be the chosen artist and thus inaugurate a dazzling career as one of the foremost book illustrators of the 1840s and 1850s.

However, Thackeray's efforts to secure a commission were eventually successful and, in 1838, he provided a set of twelve of what Henry Vizetelly describes as 'execrable illustrations' for Douglas Jerrold's *Men of Character*. Further attempts to secure work as a book illustrator were an almost total failure.[6]

Nor is the reason hard to seek. The advantages of wealth and class, the public-school and university education, proved positive handicaps in Thackeray's development as an artist. Thinking, perhaps, of his own lack of training as a painter, Thackeray could complain with some justice in *The Paris Sketch Book* that 'In England there is no school [of art] except the Academy, unless the student can afford to pay a very large sum, and place himself under the tuition of some particular artist'. In addition, the book illustrator needed a technical training to master the crafts of drawing upon boxwood blocks for the engraver and of etching his own designs upon steel or copper. This training would, in any case, have been well-nigh impossible for Thackeray to acquire, given his character and circumstances. Among notable contemporary book illustrators, George Cruikshank and Richard Doyle had artist fathers and were brought up to the trade, while Phiz had been learning the technique as an apprentice to one of London's two leading engravers, Finden, at a time when Thackeray was still studying his Greek and Latin. As a result, when he came to market his skills, Thackeray had little more to offer than his innate artistic ability for, apart from his desultory studies in Paris, he was almost completely untrained as a painter, seems to have received very little instruction in draughtsmanship, and was virtually self-taught as an etcher.

He was, however, fortunate that the same classical education which he had endured at Charterhouse was perhaps the best training which anyone with a natural gift for words could receive in respect of their meaning and use. In this sense, then, his schooldays were as much an apprenticehsip in writing as Phiz's indentures were in art. The schoolboy verses in his local Devonshire newspaper *The Western Luminary*, the undergraduate journalism and the contributions during his stay in Weimar to Ottalie von Goethe's *Chaos* were amateur steps in the professional direction inaugurated by his reviews for *Fraser's* from 1831 and by the Paris letters of 1833 for *The National Standard*. Because he had some training as a writer—and little or none as an artist—writing provided him with the independent living which art could not. Yet, if his artistic abilities were at this time insufficient to earn him a living as the illustrator of other men's books, they were enough to enable him to illustrate his own almost from the very start. Thus he was able so to develop a talent and to acquire a skill that some ten years later he was not merely one of *Punch's* leading writers, but a very useful second-string to the magazine's artists, Leech, Doyle and Henning.

If, then, art could never, as he had once hoped, provide him with an independence, it could and did most usefully supplement Thackeray's literary earnings. In cash terms this meant that he could offer Fraser *The Yellowplush Correspondence* at 'twelve guineas a sheet [of 16 pages] and a drawing for each number in which his story appears—the drawing two guineas' (letter to James Fraser, 5 March 1838). Eight years later, according o Vizetelly, Thackeray 'reckoned the text [of *Vanity Fair*], I remember at no more than twenty-five shillings a page, the two etchings at six guineas each, while, as for the few initials at the beginnings of the chapters, he threw these in'.[7] Thus any disappointment in failure to make a living as an artist was in some degree compensated by the important financial contribution which art made to his literary earnings at a time when each and every source of income was vital to him.

2 Struggle and Achievement

The years between 1837, when Thackeray and his small family returned to London, and 1846, when he could make a permanent home for his children there, were years of struggle to establish himself as a writer. His eldest daughter, Anne, had been born in London on 9 June 1837; a second daughter, Jane, was born on 9 July in the following year, but died on 14 March 1839; and his third and last child, another daughter, Harriet, was born on 27 May 1840. Then came personal tragedy: in September of that year, on a voyage to Ireland, his wife Isabella attempted to commit suicide by jumping overboard. Although Thackeray long hoped that the insanity which had

driven her to try to make away with herself was temporary, and different cures were tried at various establishments in France and Germany throughout this period, by 1845 he was forced to acknowledge that his wife was permanently insane. He brought her back to England to be cared for by a family called Bakewell in Camberwell.

Thackeray had been passionately in love with his wife, and the pain which her state caused him may be imagined. What made it even harder to bear was the separation from his daughters which the situation forced upon him. Thackeray had always been fond of children (some of his most characteristic draughtsmanship, as we shall see, was produced for their entertainment) and to be unable to have his own with him in London and to be forced to entrust them to his mother in Paris only increased his loneliness.[8]

These were added handicaps in the battle to secure his own living, pay for the medical care which his wife needed, contribute to the support of his daughters, repay those members of his family and the friends who had come to his aid at the height of the crisis and clear his stepfather's liabilities incurred when *The Constitutional* failed. Nor could he disregard the need to save something from his income, if such saving were possible, for his old age and his children's futures.

All this meant unremitting literary labour from 1838 to 1850, during which time his mainstays were *Fraser's Magazine* (1837–46) and *Punch* (1842–51). In *Fraser's* first appeared works of fiction such as *The Yellowplush Correspondence* (1837–8), *Catherine* (1839–40), *A Shabby Genteel Story* (1840), *The Great Hoggarty Diamond* (1841), *The Fitzboodle Papers* (1842–3) and *The Luck of Barry Lyndon* (1844), as well as book reviews and art criticism. *Punch* was something very different and Thackeray's contributions were different, too—short paragraphs, humorous verses, cartoons (in the modern sense), some of his best burlesques, including 'Punch's Prize Novelists' (1847), and from 28 February 1846 to 27 February 1847 'The Snobs of England', his *The Book of Snobs*.

In addition, Thackeray undertook a considerable amount of book reveiwing— John Sterling had introduced him to *The Times* in this rôle in 1837 and he wrote reveiws also for *The Morning Chronicle*, both papers printing his art criticisms as well. Other contributions appeared *inter alia*, in *The New Westminster Review*, *Bentley's Miscellany* and *The New Monthly* and *Ainsworth's Magazines*. None of this, except for what is contained in *Comic Tales and Sketches* (1841), was reprinted in separate volume form until *Vanity Fair* and its successors had made Thackeray's name. However, between *Flore et Zéphyr* in 1836 and the first appearance of *Vanity Fair* in January 1847, Thackeray published three books which in some sense closely follow the very first ideas which he had formed for combining his artistic and literary talents.

As far back as 25 February 1831, during his stay in Weimar, he was telling his mother:

> I will return to Germany, & take a survey of the woods and country of it wh: are little known—I think with a sketch-book, a note-book, & I fear still a Dictionary I could manage to concoct a book wh: would pay me for my trouble, & wh: would be a novelty in England. There are plenty of dry descriptions of public buildings, pictures views armories & so forth—but the People of Germany are not known in England, & the more I learn of them the more interesting they appear to me—Customs, & Costumes— and National Songs, stories &c with wh: the country abounds, & wh: I would be glad to learn, & the 'British Public' also I think.

Something similar occurred to him when he was in touch with Macrone over the abortive plan to illustrate Ainsworth's *Crichton*. As a postscript to the letter of January 1837 which I have already quoted, he wrote: 'Will you give me £50 20 now for the 1st edition of a book in 2 Wollums with 20 drawings entitled Rambles & Sketches in old and new Paris by   . . .' But Macrone did not bite and, although this sounds very like Thackeray's *Paris Sketch*

Book, the 1840 publication is something rather different, being a reprint of articles originally written for and first published in various magazines.[9]

However, the other two books, *The Irish Sketch Book* (1843), which went into a second edition in 1845, and *Notes of a Journey from Cornhill to Grand Cairo* (1846), certainly hark back to the original idea, the shrewd if unpretentious observations of a traveller, illustrated from his sketchbook. In the first instance Thackeray proceeded to Ireland under his own steam, in the second under that of the P & O, who paid his expenses.

By 1846 Thackeray's rising reputation enabled him to enter the Christmas book market with the first of his five works in this genre, published in each successive December from 1846 to 1850.[10]

Then, in January 1847, began the serial publication of *Vanity Fair*, Thackeray's master-work and one of the greatest European works of the imagination of the nineteenth century. It ran until June 1848 and was followed by *Pendennis*. In both cases Thackeray supplied the two full-page steel etchings needed for each monthly part-issue and designed the woodcut initial letters and vignettes printed with the text.

The publication of *Pendennis*, however, marks the end of a distinct period in Thackeray's career as an illustrator of his own writings. It was followed by *Esmond* which, to give the illusion of its being authentic eighteenth-century memoirs, was published without any illustrations and was even printed in an old-face type to add the right period flavour. Thackeray began *Esmond* in August 1851, and in December of that year there occurred the famous quarrel with *Punch* over its savage attacks upon Louis Napoleon, Thackeray's resignation from the magazine and the consequent end of nearly ten years' active literary and artistic collaboration. At this pause in Thackeray's graphic output, therefore, it may be convenient to survey his *oeuvre* to date, the historical context in which it was produced, and Thackeray's own views on illustrated books.

The first period of Thackeray's work as an illustrator coincides with one of the most interesting and certainly the most vital periods in the history of book design, when all the traditional manual skills enjoyed an Indian summer of extraordinary brilliance before they were superseded by mechanical and chemical methods of graphic reproduction. Ironically, it was one of the earliest chemical discoveries—the first successful French use of electrotypes in 1839—which gave the manual process, the woodcut, a great new lease of life, for this invention coicided with the revival in France of the woodcut as the paramount process of graphic reproduction in printed books and media where illustration is combined with letterpress.

For more than a hundred years after the first invention of printing from movable types, the relief woodcut had been most generally employed to reproduce illustrations. Even in the fifteenth century, however, the intaglio process of copperplate engraving was in use; and, by the end of the sixteenth century, it began to be ever more widely employed. During the seventeenth and eighteenth centuries it virtually ousted the woodcut as the means of illustrating all except the chap-book and the cheap ephemeral publication, despite its economic disadvantages.

Since the woodcut is a relief process like printing-type, text and illustrations can be printed together; engraving, an intaglio process, requires a separate press, so that illustrations have to be printed separately or, if they are to be integrated with the text, then the sheets have to be printed twice over —once for the text and once for the illustrations. But these disadvantages were offset by other factors. The designer depends for his success upon the engraver of a woodcut, but can himself etch or engrave the copperplate; the block for the fifteenth- and sixteenth-century woodcut was engraved with the grain, generally in pearwood, and, because it was liable to crack with use, its working life was comparatively short (at least in a fine state), whereas the copperplate,

which could be re-etched or re-engraved as the surface was worn down, was by comparison virtually indestructible; and finally and perhaps decisively, although the woodcut was capable of great delicacy and subtlety, its keynote was (and is) simplicity, whereas the copperplate could supply all the richness of engraving which Baroque taste demanded.

Thus, by the eighteenth century, the woodcut had been relegated to the chap-book, illustrating the cheap publications which printers issued to satisfy the demands of their poorer customers. This was, of course, largely a provincial market of which, naturally, provincial printers took a very large share; and it is thanks to the cultural richness of English provincial life in the eighteenth century that the revival of the woodcut is due. The method of end-grain engraving on boxwood, capable of producing a sharp and delicate image, was perfected by the North Country engraver Thomas Bewick and applied to illustrations in books issued from Newcastle-upon-Tyne in the last quarter of the eighteenth century. By the end of the century it had been taken up by William Bulmer, a printer of European renown, and he had commissioned Bewick to illustrate books produced to the highest standards of contemporary typography.

As a result, by the second decade of the nineteenth century, at a time when all things English were greatly admired by the French, the woodcut was competing upon equal terms with the copperplate as a medium of book illustration. In this Anglophile atmosphere, the great French printer and publisher, Firmin Didot, immediately appreciated both the aesthetic quality and the solid economic advantages of the woodcut. Since the French had virtually lost the art of wood-engraving, he took the initiative of inviting to Paris one of the foremost English wood-engravers, Charles Thompson, who opened his atelier as a training school for French engravers.

By the 1830s this initiative had borne fruit in a group of highly skilled French craftsmen, perfectly capable of translating on to wood the designs of the artists of the period. The result is what the French term *le livre romantique*, the romantic book, throwing over the traces of chilly classicism in a riot of woodcut borders around the pages, initial letters to open the chapters, and illustrations integrated with the text. It was a style which profoundly influenced English book design and its influence was all the more immediate because of the invention of electrotypes. These enabled an exact copy of any given woodblock to be made in metal, which not only increased enormously the effective life of the block but allowed an international trade in book illustrations to spring up.[11] Thus British readers of *The Devil on Sticks* or *Gulliver's Travels* and French readers of *Le diable boiteux* or *Les voyages de Gulliver* might be using different texts and editions of Le Sage's or Swift's classics, but they would have identical illustrations, by Tony Johannot or Grandville. The style of the romantic book therefore rapidly became international.

It was a style which Thackeray immediately appreciated when he first encountered it at its birth in Paris in the 1830s when, emphasizing the poverty of French painting, he wrote to Edward Fitzgerald on 8 October 1834:

> Yesterday at the Luxembourg I was astonished to see how bad everything was—there is not I think a single good picture among all the elite of modern French art—but then in return, the sketches in the novels, the penny magazines &c are full of talent.

Nine years later, in a letter to his publishers Chapman & Hall (cited in note 11), he suggests writing for them an article on 'Paris Almanacks' illustrated by this style of woodcut, which is, of course, the very style which he adopted to illustrate his own writing in *Punch*, a magazine consciously based upon Parisian models.

In a different context, Thackeray welcomed the style for the freshness it brought into a class of illustrated books of which he was an inveterate and trenchant critic. These were the annuals, lavish Christmas gift books, pots-pourris of verse and prose prepared specifically to match the steel engravings which were their *raison-d'etre*. A feature of his reviewing for *Fraser's Magazine* was the regular onslaught he made against them, so aptly titled in January 1839 'Our Annual Execution'. Here he remarks that

> such beautiful vapidity pervades the chief portion of the pictures submitted to the public that to remember them is sheer impossibility; we may look at them over and over again, year after year, *Scrapbook* after *Scrapbook*, and never recognize our former insipid acquaintances; so that the very best plan is this of Messrs Fisher, to change not the plates, but just the names underneath, and make Medora into Haidee, or Desdemona, or what you will.

By contrast, when it came to reviewing *Poems and Pictures* in *Fraser's* ('About a Christmas Book', December 1845) he could write that 'this book in particular, just published by Mr. Burns' was

> the very best of Christmas books. Let us say this . . . who in other days have pitilessly trampled on *Forget-me-nots*, and massacred whole galleries of *Books of Beauty*. . . . The united work of these poets and artists is very well suited to the kind and gentle Christmas season. All the verses are not good, and some of the pictures are but feeble; yet the whole impression of the volume is an exceedingly pleasant one. The solemn and beautiful forms of the figures; the sweet soothing cadences and themes of the verse, affect one like music. Pictures and songs are surrounded by beautiful mystical arabesques, waving and twining round each page. Every now and then you light upon one which is so pretty, it looks as if you had put a flower between the leaves.

He went on to repeat his praise at the end of a highly appreciative review of Richard Doyle's illustrations of *The Fairy Ring* in *The Morning Chronicle* of 26 December 1845 by remarking that *Poems and Pictures* was a book 'than which English typography has produced nothing more beautiful'.

Poems and Pictures is a romantic book, but in the style developed in Germany[12] (Thackeray remarks that 'the charming *Lieder und Bilder* of the Dusseldorf painters has, no doubt, given the idea of the work') rather than in direct imitation of the French style. Perhaps, then, a more pertinent example of Thackeray's taste is to be found in his notice of Charles Lever's *Saint Patrick's Eve* in *The Morning Chronicle* of 3 April 1845. The illustrations by Phiz make it one of the most attractive examples of the smaller English romantic book and, while Thackeray found plenty to criticize in the text, he certainly liked the illustrations, writing that 'great praise must be bestowed upon the charming, faithful and picturesque designs with which Mr Brown [*sic*] has illustrated this brilliant little volume'.

If Thackeray was in general so sympathetic to the style of the romantic book, he also found the subject matter of so much of its illustration congenial to his taste and consonant with his own literary aims. To consider visual Romanticism in terms solely of Scott's historical novels or Byron's exotic orientalism is to ignore the inherent realism of the founding father, Wordsworth. Admittedly his realism is rural and finds its visual counterpart in the realist but gradually sentimentalized vignettes of English country life from Bewick to Birket Foster, while the artists of the French romantic book focus upon the realities of urban life. Thackeray's essay, 'Caricature and Lithography in Paris', first published in *The London and Westminster Review* in 1839 and then reprinted in *The Paris Sketch Book*, is a wholehearted and surprisingly early appreciation of one of the greatest of these artists, Honoré Daumier, and of his satirical series *Les Robert Macaires*. Nor does Thackeray neglect to pay tribute to Phillipon, publisher not merely of so much of this satiric art but also of *Charivari*, the model for *Punch*.

Thackeray was associated with *Punch* from the outset, and most of his best graphic work is to be found there, for this is the young, unruly, iconoclastic *Punch*, not the respectable paterfamilias it afterwards became. It thus suited Thackeray very well, for while he was not the first radical to earn his bread-and-butter by contributing to the right-wing press (in his case *Fraser's* and *The Times*), his own strongly radical and even republican political views were much better reflected in the short-lived *Constitutional;* hence he must have found the atmosphere of the radical *Punch* extremely congenial. Certainly he proved to be one of its most distinguished contributors and, while 'The Snobs of England' marks the high point of their association, his 'Travels in London', 'Mr Brown's Letters' and, in particular, 'A Little Dinner at Timmins's' all provide keen portrayal of and satiric comment on contemporary mores, while in 'Punch's Prize Novelists' he is in his happiest vein of parody.

To all these he contributed his own illustrations and, in fact, became a *Punch* artist in his own right. Apart from individual cartoons, including the series of seven 'Authors' Miseries', he supplied a large number of small cuts for use as initial letters, of which that for his own 'On Clerical Snobs' (plate 57) is a typical example. Moreover, the work for *Punch* shows how he developed into a very competent artist. The small initials stand comparison with those provided by Richard Doyle (who very clearly influenced their design), the cartoons (for example, plates 31, 43 and 44) are not so patently inferior to those of John Leech at his run-of-the-mill, and the illustrations which he supplied for his own articles (for example, plates 30, 42 and 47) match the work of Archibald Henning. All three of these artists exerted a beneficial influence upon Thackeray, and Thackeray by no means disgraces himself in their company. Yet perhaps the most interesting thing about his work for *Punch* is that the woodcuts, despite the obvious influences, are still highly individual and manage to catch the spontaneous style of the pen-sketches with which he delighted to ornament his letters.

It is not unreasonable to suggest that this success was due in large measure to the fact that Thackeray was submitting his designs regularly and over a period of nearly ten years to the same printing house and probably to the same engraver. Indeed, the rôle of the craftsman is crucial, for the engraver always intervenes between the artist's original design and the image of the woodcut on the printed page. With a skilled engraver and an artist who really understands the medium, the distortion is so slight as to be virtually non-existent. Yet even artists who were thoroughly competent draughtsmen or painters in oils or watercolours might well fail to master the medium of the woodcut. Indeed, Henry Vizetelly, one of the most skilful printers of woodcuts in the 1840s, says in his memoirs that the distinguished illustrator Clarkson Stanfield 'like many other painters, found the difficulty of drawing on the box-wood block with the necessary neatness and precision almost insurmountable'. How much more, then, must Thackeray have depended upon a sympathetic engraver to translate his design and I believe he found one for his *Punch* woodcuts.

This becomes apparent when we compare them with the woodcuts in his books. The engraver responsible for the vignettes in both *The Paris* and *The Irish Sketch Books* was Landells, a highly skilled but somewhat old-fashioned craftsman. Given Thackeray's inexperience, and hence his inability to convey his intentions to the engraver through his drawing upon the block, the engraver was compelled to interpret those intentions and, if the studio were old-fashioned, Thackeray might find himself translated into a somewhat outmoded artistic idiom. This is what seems to have happened in *The Paris Sketch Book* where, of the vignettes (of which four are given as examples in plates 21–4), only 'Hotel Touts' (plate 21) approaches Thackeray's spontaneous style. The same is true of *The Irish Sketch Book*, from which I have chosen those vignettes (plates 32–7) which I believe come closest to Thackeray's originals. However,

among them, I have included as typical of the majority of the cuts 'The Landlord' (plate 32), finely engraved in the style of the 1820s, to show why Thackeray could write to his mother in March 1843 that 'all the Irish blocks are spoiled'. Although the woodcuts for *Notes of a Journey from Cornhill to Cairo* were placed in Vizetelly's hands and although he gets much closer to what must have been Thackeray's intentions (the self-portrait, plate 54, approaches the marginal sketch of the Thackerean letter), there seems still to be some uneasiness, due to lack of intuitive understanding between artist and engraver, betrayed by the rather old-fashioned style of 'The Horsedealers' (plate 51) and 'Zuleika' (plate 53).

Vizetelly himself recalls that

Mr Thackeray was at this period painfully cognisant of his lack of technical skill as an etcher, and he asked me to find him someone who would etch the frontispiece to the Cairo volume from his water-colour sketch. I gave the job to a young fellow in our employment called Thwaites, who subsequently put a number of Thackeray's sketches for 'Mrs Perkins's Ball' on the wood, and touched up the hands and other matters in those subjects drawn on the blocks by Thackeray himself. The annexed note evidently refers to some of the drawings made by Thwaites.

Dear Sir,—I return the drawings after making a few alterations in them. Present Mr Titmarch's compliments to your talented young man, and say M. A. T. would take it as a favour if he would kindly confine his improvements to the Mulligan's and Mrs Perkins's other guests' extremities. In your young gentleman's otherwise praiseworthy corrections of my vile drawing, a certain *je ne sais quoi*, which I flatter myself exists in the original sketches, seems to have given him the slip, and I have tried in vain to recapture it. Somehow I prefer my own Nuremburg dolls to Mr Thwaite's super-fine wax models.— Yours,   W.M.T.   Sept. 13.

From the little services in this way which I had been able to render Mr Thackeray, I had become rather intimate with him, and while the drawings for 'Perkins's Ball' and others of his Christmas books printed by me, were in progress, I saw a good deal of him, for he was almost as fastidious, as I afterwards found Mr Ruskin to be, in regard to the manner in which his sketches were transferred to the wood.

This extract raises some very interesting points to be taken into account when we consider Thackeray's steel etchings but, as far as the woodcuts are concerned, it tends to confirm my view that the engraver made corrections either when transferring sketches to the wood or else when he came to engrave the drawings which Thackeray himself had already made upon the blocks. Vizetelly describes Thackeray as being 'fastidious' and clearly there was not that full sympathy between the novelist and young Thwaites which we presume existed with the *Punch* engraver. This would explain why the illustrations for *Mrs Perkin's Ball* (plates 68–73), *Our Street* (plates 81–5) and *The Kickleburys on the Rhine* (plates 166–7), despite the generic differences between a design for a full-page plate and one to be integrated into the double column of a much larger format, may lack some of the spontaneity of the *Punch* woodcuts. This is not true (and this further confirms my thesis) of the woodcut initials which appear in *Vanity Fair* and *Pendennis*. Both books were printed by Bradbury & Evans, the publishers of *Punch;* and to the dinner given in July 1848 by Thackeray and his *Punch* colleagues to mark the completion of *Vanity Fair* Mr Bradbury was invited. An invitation was also sent to William Joyce, a wood-engraver of Bolt Court, Fleet Street, who was presumably responsible for the woodcuts in the novel and, given the interconnexion, for the *Punch* illustrations as well. However, Vizetelly's remarks about Thackeray's inexperience as an etcher rouse the most interesting speculations, although they cannot be taken at face value when we consider Thackeray's output in this medium up to this date.

His feeble undergraduate efforts, an example of which is given as plate 10, show his early interest in the medium, but it seems unlikely that he thought of practising the craft commercially until about 1835 when, as we have seen his efforts to etch on copper proved unsuccessful and he failed to secure commissions either to illustrate Ainsworth's *Crichton* or to supply a series of topographical plates. His arrangement with James Fraser for the illustrations to *The Yellowplush Correspondence* implies that drawings, which the publisher was to engrave, were to be supplied, and this is confirmed by the confession Thackeray made in a letter to his wife of 14 March 1838 that he had been 'up very early yesterday finishing a very bad drawing for Fraser.—I almost hope he won't insert it.'

Catherine followed *The Yellowplush Correspondence* in *Fraser's* from May 1839 to February 1840, and was illustrated by steel etchings in the same simple and somewhat crude style. There is, however, a greater confidence in the drawing (cf plates 17 and 18) which may in all probability be due to the fact that Thackeray himself etched them rather than supplied drawings for the engraver as before.

In 1840 John Macrone published *The Paris Sketch Book* with full-page etchings which show a still further advance in the simple line technique (see plates 19, 20, 25, and 26). Again there is no evidence for or against Thackeray's responsibility for their etching, but the likelihood is that they are his. He obviously needed the money and he must clearly have acquired practical experience of etching somewhere if he were to undertake the extensive series needed for *Vanity Fair* and *Pendennis* (thirty for the former and forty-eight for the latter). Most probably *Yellowplush* was the exception to the rule, because he was at that time fulfilling one of his very few commissions as a book illustrator—to supply a set of twelve etchings for Douglas Jerrold's *Men of Character*. In the circumstances, it seems most unlikely that Thackeray would have merely supplied design for these twelve etchings, and, however second-rate and derivative the actual plates may be, they do show that he had made some technical progress. They are a link between his undergraduate efforts and the etchings in *Catherine* and *The Paris Sketch Book*.

More interesting are the etchings (see plates 27–9) which Thackeray provided to illustrate the two-volume collection *Comic Tales and Sketches*, published in 1841. The first volume, with frontispiece and five plates, contains *The Yellowplush Correspondence;* in Volume II are gathered 'Some Passages in the Life of Major Gahagan' and 'The Bedford Row Conspiracy', which had previously appeared in *The New Monthly Magazine;* 'The Professor', reprinted from *Bentley's Miscellany;* and 'Stubbs's Calendar'. None of the stories from the magazines had been illustrated on first publication, while 'Stubbs's Calendar' had been contributed to George Cruikshank's *Comic Almanac*. Thackeray provides four plates for 'Major Gahagan' and one each for 'The Professor' and 'The Bedford Row Conspiracy'. The plates for *Yellowplush* illustrate different subjects from those supplied for first publication in *Fraser's*. What is more, they show considerable technical and artistic advance on anything which Thackeray had hitherto produced, being extremely delicate and giving the impression of being sepia drawings. Assuming that they are Thackeray's unaided work, there is no reason to suppose that four years later he would not have been perfectly capable, had he so wished, of etching a copy of his watercolour as frontispiece to his *Notes of a Journey from Cornhill to Cairo*, although between 1841 and 1845 he had been designing almost exclusively for wood-engraving.

A far more likely explanation is that he simply had neither the time not the inclination to make a copy. Not only was he in all probability at work on *Vanity Fair* (the first chapters had been sent to Colburn in May) but, in the autumn of 1845, when this incident may be presumed to have occurred, he had the very painful task of bringing his wife to England in October and of seeing her safely installed with Mrs Bakewell in Camberwell. Vizetelly's perversion of the facts may thus be explained as the all-too-natural wish to score in retrospect off the great and famous. It is quite inconsistent with the production between January 1847, just over a year later, and December 1850 of the bulk of Thackeray's etched work, the hard-ground etchings for *Vanity Fair* and *Pendennis* and the soft-ground etchings for *The Great Hoggarty Diamond* and *Doctor Birch and his Young Friends*.

1848 had been the year of revolutions in Germany, and it was considered impolitic to publish *The Kickleburys on the Rhine*, the Christmas book planned for December of that year. Instead, and at somewhat short notice, Thackeray produced *Doctor Birch and his Young Friends*. Apparently the original intention had been to illustrate it with woodcuts (as the other Christmas books were illustrated) and the change to soft-ground etching seems to have followed Thackeray's letter of 25 October 1848 to his publisher Edward Chapman, in which he reported:

> I have brought a lot of blocks into the country to do them: but I believe that the soft point would be the thing after all, with the aid of my friend Marvy.[13] . . . I am sure we shall do them better than the wood—I could do 4 of a day easily, and he would have them bitten in no time . . .

The illustrations (plates 126–7) are agreeable, and it was perhaps Thackeray's pleasure at the results—he had considered the roughs 'good odd & new'—which led him to employ the same technique to illustrate the reprint in book form of *The Great Hoggarty Diamond* in the following year. The plates, to my taste, are in their ensemble some of the most attractive which Thackeray produced, while 'The Common Lot' (plate 135) has a dignity and pathos inspired by the similar death of the Thackeray's second child: the whole forms a charming little book.

How far its success is due to the presumed collaboration of so experienced an etcher as Marvy to undertake the 'biting-in' it is impossible to determine. At least they were not so rushed as the plates for *Doctor Birch*, for in December 1848, within days of its publication, Thackeray had written to Edward Chapman that the last two were unfinished. In addition, by 1849 when Thackeray etched the plates for *The Great Hoggarty Diamond*, having completed the set for *Vanity Fair* and begun those for *Pendennis*, he had become so adept in the medium that he could boast in a letter to Mrs Brookfield of 24 July 1849 that he had finished his instalment of *Pendennis* 'and done my two plates, which only took two hours'.

These were hard-ground etchings, and he refers simply to the initial process of transferring the design to the wax and of exposing with his needle the areas to be etched. As in the case of the soft-ground etchings, the rôle of the craftsman who bit-in these designs would be crucial. We know that Doyle's etchings for *The Newcomes* (1854) were bitten-in by Robert Young, and it is conceivable that Young's connexion with Bradbury & Evans extended back to *Vanity Fair* and *Pendennis*. If this is so, Thackeray was fortunate since Young had set up in this trade in 1834 with Hablot Knight Browne ('Phiz') and had worked in close association with this master of the steel etching ever since.

3 The Later Years

Completion of the illustrations for *Pendennis* marks a period in Thackeray's career as an illustrator. Almost simultaneously he cut his connexion with *Punch;* his next novel, *Esmond*, was not illustrated; and its successor, *The Newcomes*, was to be illustrated by another artist—Richard Doyle. Thereafter —with two important exceptions, *The Virginians* and *The Rose and the Ring*— Thackeray was less and less inclined to exploit his artistic talents to supplement his earnings as a writer.

It is to some extent a question of scale. Thackeray, while he applied the highest standards,[14] had adopted the profession of letters as a means of earning his livelihood.

At the start of his career the money which he could earn as an illustrator must have been a substantial proportion of his total income. The success of *Vanity Fair* meant that thereafter writing was infinitely more lucrative than drawing; in any case, there was a marked difference between the drawings which he made for his own amusement and those which he prepared for publication. As his daughter Anne, later Lady Ritchie, wrote in her preface to *The Orphan of Pimlico*,

> the hours which he spent upon his drawing blocks and sketch books brought no fatigue or weariness; they were of endless interest to him, and rested him when he was tired. It was only when he came to etch upon steel, or to draw for the engraver upon wood, that he complained of effort and want of ease . . .

Success in his chosen profession meant relief from this tedious labour although, as we shall see, he could never wholly break himself of the habit.

Success, too, provided fresh goals for his ambitions and new means of achieving them for, having assured himself and his family of a livelihood, he could now think of providing for the futures of his dependents—his two daughters and his wife. Although Isabella Thackeray was hopelessly deranged —her madness took the form of a carefree infantilism—she enjoyed excellent health and gave every indication of outliving her husband, as in the event she did, by some thirty years. Thackeray, however, must have been all too conscious of his own indifferent state of health. He had been critically ill in the autumn of 1849; throughout his life he suffered from the venereal complaint which he had contracted as a young man, as well as from his almost pathological over-indulgence in food and drink; and then in December 1854, while working in Rome upon his novel *The Newcomes*, he was seriously ill once more. It took him two months to recover from the immediate effects of the illness, and it left him in indifferent health for the rest of his life.

He had, therefore, little time to reach his financial goal, but was able to achieve it thanks to his success in what turned out to be the extremely rewarding rôle of lecturer. In the summer of 1851 he gave his lectures on *The English Humourists* in London, repeating them in Oxford and Cambridge and in Scotland in the winter, and in London again early in 1852. In the autumn of that year he lectured in Manchester and Liverpool before sailing for North America, where he carried *The English Humourists* from New York to Savannah between November 1852 and April 1853.

The success of this tour surpassed all expectations and, although on his return to England he was next engaged between 1853 and 1855 in writing and publishing *The Newcomes*, he immediately followed the novel with a fresh series of lectures, on *The Four Georges*, which he first delivered on a more extended tour of the United States of America from October 1855 to March 1856 and then repeated in the British Isles between November 1856 and May 1857. To read the letters written during these periods is to appreciate the energy which Thackeray put into this exhausting work and the driving force behind this killing effort—the need to provide for his dependents.

Knowing this cause, we may excuse the patent delight, the glee with which Thackeray almost gloats over the way in which the money flowed in from audiences on both sides of the Atlantic. Indeed, we may share the pleasure and the sense of achievement he so obviously felt when his writing, but more especially his lecturing, enabled him to restore the inheritance which had vanished when he was a young man—a goal towards which he had deliberately aimed—and to be able to leave to his daughters and their mother more than his father had bequeathed to him. This was no unworthy ambition and no mean achievement, possible only through his success in his chosen profession, as writer and lecturer and as the moving spirit behind *The Cornhill Magazine*. Of this he was the first and very successful editor, from its inception until his resignation in March 1862, within two years of his death.

The break with *Punch* and the prior engagements of the lecturer conceal what I believe to be Thackeray's natural inclination to withdraw from book illustration. His publishers, however, do seem to have expected him to have continued in the rôle of author-illustrator, and this raised the problem, on his return from a Continental holiday with his daughters in the summer of 1853, of reconciling the writing and illustrating of his new novel, *The Newcomes*, with his wish to take his daughters to winter in Rome. Fortunately, he was able to solve his dilemma by entrusting the illustrations of the book to Richard Doyle, whose work he had long admired.[15] Doyle had been for many years his associate on *Punch* and, when illness laid Thackeray low in 1849, had illustrated his Christmas book, *Rebecca and Rowena*. Yet, although he had been able to substitute the artist of his choice, the freed slave still seems to have hankered after his chains. As he wrote to his mother on 1 September 1853, 'I have just arranged with R. Doyle to do the pictures for my new book; and now that it is agreed on feel almost sorry that I am not to do them myself; but it will be a great weight off my mind and I can now move Withersumever I will.' Nor was freedom of movement the only motive for, as he wrote to his friend B. W. Proctor at about the same time, 'there was more than one good reason for giving Doyle that job. But the chief reason was—well if you can serve your friend and yourself too, aren't you lucky?'

Although the decision had been made, the regrets still lingered and, on 23 September, Thackeray wrote to his mother that 'Doyle has been 3 weeks doing the engravings [for the first number of *The Newcomes*] and they are not so good as mine'. Confirming his opinion—but was his tongue not slightly in his cheek?—in a letter four days later to his American friend Mrs Baxter, he wrote that he and his daughters were 'agreed that the pictures Mr Doyle is doing for my book, are not so good as my own—What would life be without grumbling?'

Yet, by the time the novel had run half its course and Thackeray was in Paris on his way back to London, he had reached a juster appreciation of Doyle's work, writing to Percival Leigh on 12 April 1854:

I have seen for the first time the engravings of the Newcomes some of wh: I like very much indeed. Why, Doyle ought to bless the day that put the etching needle into his hand. I'm sure he'll be able to do great things with it. He does beautifully and easily what I wanted to do and can't. There are capital bits in almost all the etchings. Some of the wood-blox have been awfully mangled in the engraving, but Gandish and young Moss (in 2 places) are admirable.

Although the experiment had proved successful, it was not repeated with Thackeray's next novel, *The Virginians*, for one very good reason: Thackeray was an historian[16] and, as such, had a keen eye for historical accuracy. This is the one good aspect of his plates for *Catherine;* indeed it is precisely upon this point that he takes Phiz to task in an otherwise favourable review of his illustrations to Charles Lever's *Our Mess* in the February 1844 issue of *Fraser's Magazine*. Despite the fact that the novel is set in the French Revolutionary Wars, all the characters except Napoleon wear the military finery of the 1840s 'and a study of the admirable sketches of Raffet and Charlet would have given the designer a better notion of the costume of the soldiery of the consulate than that which he has adopted'.[17]

As in his earlier novels, the illustrations (see plates 179–88) of *The Virginians* comprised woodcut initials and full-page steel etchings. In some sense Thackeray's amateur status as an etcher makes his work in this medium (with the exception of the plates for *Men of Character*) slightly atypical of the period since he could not work them so heavily as could the acknowledged masters of the medium. Thus he was less affected by the shift in taste which gathered speed during the 1850s. Essentially this was the ousting by the German-influenced romantics —Thackeray had detected this influence in

the 1845 *Poems and Pictures*—of the French-influenced woodcut designers and native etchers, of whom Thackeray was one. This produced the typical 'Sixties Book' illustration, with its deceptively simple and rather statuesque if not static lines. Thackeray had no need to simplify his etchings— although etching was being ousted by the woodcut in full-page plates—to meet the taste for the simpler line, although by contrast he had to elaborate his woodcuts (see plates 182–7) to match the richer effects of 'high art'. It therefore seems probable that his realization that his style was going out of fashion combined with all the other motives to restrict his work as a book illustrator.

It was not until three years after the publication of *The Virginians*, though, that he ran into any serious difficulties on this score. In January 1860 the first number of *The Cornhill Magazine*, under Thackeray's editorship, began to serialize his new novel, *Lovel the Widower*. Unfortunately, the other novel being concurrently serialized was Anthony Trollope's *Framley Parsonage*, superbly illustrated in the 'Sixties style by John Millais. Thackeray was too good a critic to be unaware not only that Millais was infinitely his superior as a draughtsman but that the difference was made all the more cruelly apparent by Thackeray's old-fashioned style. The solution was for the engraver to 'improve' the design Thackeray supplied, either on or when transferring it to the wood. How unsatisfactory this expedient was can be seen from the example of a full-page plate which I have chosen, 'Bessy's Spectacles' (plate 189); nor was it any more satisfactory when the next novel, *Philip*, came to be serialized in 1861. This moved the publisher, George Smith, to introduce the promising young artist, Fred Walker, to 'improve' Thackeray's design.[18] He is certainly responsible for touching up the woodcuts illustrating the third and fourth instalments of the novel, but whether his hand can be seen in the first two is uncertain. What is sure is that he rebelled against the work and threatened to walk out unless he were allowed to illustrate the rest of the novel entirely on his own.

To this Thackeray was happy to accede (although he continued to design the initials) and the remaining full-page plates are by Walker, who was also commissioned to illustrate Thackeray's last, unfinished, novel *Denis Duval*. Yet, however good these illustrations are, however much better the draughtsmanship, we are, I feel, bound to regret them since they translate us straight from the raffish world of the 1840s which Thackeray made so much his own into a stiflingly respectable mid-Victorian milieu. This is best typified by Walker's plate 'Judith and Holophernes', depicting Little Sister who, having made him drunk on brandy and water, is about to chloroform that broken-down, boozy, grubby clergyman, the Reverend Tufton Hunt, so as to pick his pocket of the forged bill of exchange which will ruin Philip. From Thackeray's text one visualizes Hunt as the seedy alcoholic which he is; but in Walker's woodcut it looks more as if his respectable housekeeper had come in to straighten the dear old rector who has slid down his chair while taking a post-prandial nap. Thackeray's pen was too sharp for Walker's world.

This world, the world of the 1850s and 1860s, exhibits a most striking change from the two decades which had preceded it. It shows a sudden and sharp swing away from the acceptance of that possibility of violent and revolutionary change in society which had come to a head in 1848, to an equal acceptance that society had in fact changed from within. This was not wholly due to the failure of those revolutionary movements after 1848 but, certainly in England, to the feeling that society was becoming better and more just, curing its old abuses without the need to tear everything down and start afresh. Nor was this an unreasonable attitude: the good old vices still flourished, but High Society had taken a more moral tone which, if adopted hypocritically by some, was still a genuine

expression by others of a higher ideal. This was exemplified by a wholly new attitude in government, both at home and, more especially, in India, prudent, responsible trusteeship gradually replacing wholesale jobbery and plunder.

This change of climate profoundly affected Thackeray as a man of letters. I have suggested that financial motives probably turned him from writing to lecturing in the 1850s; it may also have been his response to the new atmosphere— if you are a professional satirist, how do you react to a society which is apparently heeding its prophets and genuinely attempting to mend its ways? In some sense your occupation is gone. This is particularly true of somebody like Thackeray, whose satire is born not of misanthropy but of a genuine love of humanity; who forbears to attack clerical snobs because of his respect for the devotion of the vast majority of clergymen and dislike for the glee with which the few backsliders are pilloried. In fact, he conveys the changed atmosphere very well in his essay on John Leech's *Pictures of Life and Character* in *The Quarterly Review* of December 1854, when he contrasts mid-Victorian with Regency England.

How savage the satire was—how fierce the assault—what garbage hurled at opponents— what foul blows hit—what language of Billingsgate flung! Fancy a party at a country-house now looking over Woodward's facetiae or some of Gilray's comicalities, or the slatternly Saturnalia of Rowlandson! Whilst we live, we must laugh, and have folks make us laugh. We cannot afford to lose Satyr with his pipe and dances and gambols. But we have washed, combed, clothed and taught the rogue good manners: or rather, let us say, he has learned them himself; for he is of nature soft and kindly, and he has put aside his mad pranks and tipsy habits; and, frolicsome always, he has become harmless, smitten into shame by the pure presence of our women and the sweet confiding smiles of our children.

The change is exemplified, Thackeray maintains, by *Punch*, of which Leech[19] is the mainstay, no longer 'earning a precarious livelihood by the cracking of wild jokes, the singing of ribald songs', but 'combed, washed, neatly clothed, and perfectly presentable'. Although there may be a hint of regret for this altered state of affairs, Thackeray is perfectly genuine in his acceptance of it and in his admiration for Leech as a chronicler of society, praising the realism of his *Pictures* and hailing him as 'the social historian of the nineteenth century'.

However, the path from social satirist to social historian was not one along which Thackeray could follow his old friend. As his preface to *Pendennis* shows, he felt constrained by the taboo against mention of sexual irregularity in the characters of any but the villains of novels. It is perhaps this feeling of constraint which makes him uneasy with the very medium in which he had worked so successfully. He was clearly dissatisfied with his performance as a novelist in *The Newcomes; The Virginians* is a sorry sequel to *Esmond; Philip*, despite some fine passages, is a clumsy work with a perfunctory dénouement; only in the small scale of *Lovel the Widower* are the old mastery and bite. How far these changes are subconscious, how far the conscious response to the expression of public taste,[20] is another matter. Quite possibly Thackeray changed his approach to writing to fit the new world of the 1860s as he attempted to alter his romantic style in book illustration to meet the popularity of 'high art'.

This is, however, to trespass into literary criticism, and his review of Leech is a reminder that one important side of Thackeray's art has so far received no mention. Both this essay and his earlier appreciation of George Cruikshank are particularly interesting from the references in the one to the delight in Cruikshank's work which Thackeray gained as a boy, and in the other to the good fortune of the Victorian child in having so many delightful picture books by contrast with the poverty in that respect of his own childhood. Indeed, one of his own most endearing and enduring masterpieces is that 'fire-side panto-mime for great and small children', *The Rose and the Ring*, his Christmas book for 1854. Its origins are well known—the Twelfth Night card-characters first cut out for his own children's amusement and then converted to the personages of a story told to lighten the convalescence of the daughter of their American sculptor neighbour in Rome, Edith Story, to whom the book is dedicated.

It is but one in a long line of entertainments which his talents produced for the amusement of children. As a young man in Weimar, he recalled in a letter of 18 April 1855 to G. H. Lewes, 'My delight in those days was to make caricatures for children. I was touched to find that they were remembered, and some even kept until the present time; and very proud to be told, as a lad, that the great Goethe had looked at some of them.' Later, when first living in Paris, he prepared for Edward Torre, the son of friends whom he used to visit at Choisy le Roi, *Simple Melodies*, six leaves of rhymes with his accompanying pen-sketches and, around the same time, for Edward Chadwick, son of acquaintances at Sherborne in Dorset, what was published in 1929 as *The Thackeray Alphabet* (plates 7 and 8). All share with *The Rose and the Ring* the humour, the realism, the detail and the love of the grotesque which Thackeray shared with the lucky young recipient of his books.

When Bulbo tears his hair (plate 172) the locks really do fly; and, when the poor fellow is shown looking out of the window of his cell on the morning of his execution, he really is 'on top of a hat-box, on top of a chair, on top of his bed, on top of his table'—and you can see his face at the window and the file of soldiers all ready to lead him off to the scaffold (plate 178). Nor is this all: when, earlier in the story, Giglio knocks King Valoroso's nose crooked with a warming-pan, sure enough, in the next cut the royal nose is as crooked as can be (plate 173). And how magnificently the enraged Count Hogginarmo kicks his two poor negroes flying (plate 176) . . . But why enumerate? If you share my delight in the book, you too will think that Mrs Oliphant was far too cool when she wrote in *Blackwood's Magazine* in January 1855:

> Mr Titmarsh has never before produced so pleasant a picture-book, nor one whose pictures were so worthy of the text. These illustrations are greatly superior to all their predecessors by the same hand; they are so good that the artist is fairly entitled to rank with the author in this pleasant production . . .

4 Conclusions

Although the contemporary reviews of Thackeray's work are liable to the corruptions of literary politics, they must be taken into account in any assessment of Thackeray's work as an illustrator, and indeed they do tend to isolate certain elements in Thackeray's art, as significant now as then. This should therefore be borne in mind in the brief extracts which follow, starting with *The Paris Sketch Book*, published in July 1840.

Writing at that time to his friend B. W. Proctor, Thackeray remarked: 'I'm afraid Forster is right about the badness of the drawings; everyone agrees with him but the Spectator and the author.' For *The Spectator* had commented: 'His etchings are masterly and distinguished by grotesque drollery, of a caustic kind, that is shown to advantage in hitting off the expressions of villains and their dupes.'

Nor, despite what Thackeray says, was *The Spectator* alone in its praise. *The Times*, for example, wrote that the illustrations contained 'less caricature than could be expected from a draughtsman who is so obviously imbued with a vigorous taste for raillery, and strong power of seeing and describing the ridiculous'; while *The Examiner* singled out the etching of Ludovicus Rex (plate 26) as 'incomparably the best design: a design indeed, which, for the amount of reflexion and fine thinking that is in it, would scarce have been unworthy of Mr Titmarsh's namesake'. But this is laying it on too thick—Titmarsh is but a self-styled

Michelangelo — and the reviewer redresses the balance by commenting: 'Of Mr Titmarsh's own deisgns generally, it will perhaps be enough to say, that the fun and humourous character that are in them plead with good effect against their sins of drawing.'

Much the same attitude was taken by the reviewer of his next book in *Ainsworth's Magazine* in May 1843 who, after a generally favourable notice of *The Irish Sketch Book*, added:

> In this manner, we had sagaciously pronounced Mr M. A. Titmarsh to be considerably more of an author than artist, until our eyes had feasted on the illustrative Irishmen appropriately adorning these pages, when we found him to be alike vigorous, original, and true, in both characters— independent in both of the ordinary rules of art.

However, recognition of the author-artist status could be a double-edged compliment, as when J. R. Findlay reveiwed *Pendennis* in *The Scotsman* of 18 December 1850 and wrote:

> Mr Thackeray is his own illustrator, and his quaint and finely characteristic etchings abound in Hogarth-like touches. They convey an impression of their being scraps and pencillings from the portfolio of an eminent and able artist, as without doubt they are, though the artist works with the pen rather than the brush.

But this is to anticipate: *The Spectator*, always a friend, duly praised the illustrations to *Notes of a Journey from Cornhill to Grand Cairo* in a review of 24 January 1846, saying:

> The "pencillings" of this little volume are as lively as the letter-press: they really *illustrate* —placing before the reader's eye just those points that must be illustrated visibly. The frontispiece [plate 48] for instance lowers the romance of the East to the level of Brighton or Hyde Park. The wood-cut sketches are remarkable for always bringing out the points of character forcibly and humourously.

With this favourable review, however, *The New Monthly Magazine* disagreed, unkindly commenting in the issue for January 1846 that in one vignette 'Zuleika [plate 53] . . . looks out from behind the wooden lattice, as if she were in the last stage of the plague, instead of casting amorous glances at our traveller.'

With the exception of *Pendennis*, the books in question, and in particular the two travel books, are decorated rather than illustrated: what then of the first major work *Vanity Fair*, with its greater and more sustained volume of illustration drawn from the imagination, rather than the life?

On 22 July 1848, in a long and not entirely favourable review, *The Spectator* observed:

> As usual with works of fiction published periodically, *Vanity Fair* is profusely illustrated with wood-cuts and etchings representing the persons and incidents of the text, by Mr Thackeray himself. If only passable or of average merit, they would be creditable, as arguing the possession of a double art: but they strike us as exhibiting powers akin to the literary abilities of the author, besides possessing this further quality: the spirit of the scene and character—the idiosyncracy of the persons—is more thoroughly entered into and presented to the reader than is common with professional artists.

The September 1848 issue of *Fraser's Magazine* was more specific:

> We ought to say something about the illustrations of our artist-author, for he gathers laurels in both fields. The humour of the plates is broad and sketchy, and full of the same cynical spirit which pervades the text. The characterisation is equally keen and striking. Becky is especially excellent; and it is only when Mr. Thackeray goes out of his satiric pleasanteries that he misses his accustomed success. The tender, drooping Amelia, is made to simper and look wretchedly lackadaisical; but the grotesque Dobbin, the surly Osborne, the radiant O'Dowd, are all capital and hit off at the top of their peculiarities with a bold and brilliant pencil.

Even these few contemporary reviews bring out what I feel to be Thackeray's main characteristics as a book illustrator. They recognize his amateur status, although it is that of an amateur well able to hold his place in a professional team; they admit the variable quality of his draughtsmanship, less evident but still present in his later etchings, horribly plain in the early etchings for *The Paris Sketch Book* and, especially, *The Yellowplush Correspondence* and *Catherine;* they appreciate his virtues, the ability to catch a likeness ('the illustrative Irishmen'), his humour, and his talent for caricature, satire and burlesque; and *The Spectator* stresses the real importance of the illustrations as being the author's personal realizations of the creatures of his imagination—distorted at times, perhaps, by his technical inadequacies, but only slightly and certainly less than had they been seen through the eyes of another. Yet, perceptive though *The Spectator* critic is, he needs to be complemented by Thackeray's self-criticism.[21]

For this is one of the novelist's most admirable traits, that his sharp, satiric eye was never blinded by self-complacency. He was too good an art-critic, with too just an appreciation of draughtsmanship, ever to be satisfied with his own efforts or to accept mere conventional compliments upon his work. Thus, writing to L. A. Adolphus on 11 May 1848, the day after Adolphus had, at the annual dinner of the Royal Literary Fund, spoken of the brilliance of Thackerays' writing and praised 'the congenial labours of his pencil', the novelist could retort that 'regarding the drawings I know you are wrong, for they are tenth or twentieth rate performances having meaning perhaps but a ludicrous badness of execution'.

In this he was, perhaps, being too severe with himself and yet, as we have seen in his comments upon Doyle's illustrations to *The Newcomes*, he was always acutely conscious of the disparity between conception and realization. Undoubtedly Thackeray's lack of technical training was to blame, It shows particularly in his etchings, and made his old friend Dr John Brown regretfully observe that 'if he had been apprenticed to Rainbach, the engraver, the English people might have had another and in some ways subtler Hogarth'. All too probably it was this awareness of his disability which inhibited Thackeray in the way which we have seen his daughter describe in her preface to *The Orphan of Pimlico*. The passage quoted continues, 'we often used to wish that his drawings could be given as they were first made, without the various transmigrations of wood and steel, and engravers' toil and printers' ink.'

In 1876 she published *The Orphan*, which reproduces photographically that story and a number of her father's other pen-sketches from the manuscripts, in proof of her contention. The sample which I have chosen (plate 9), together with a bare half-dozen from among the thousands of pen-drawings which enliven his correspondence (plates 1–6), show, all too inadequately I fear, something of Thackeray's extraordinary facility when sketching for his own amusement. It was this quality which so impressed Thomas Carlyle, who remarked in conversation with Gavin Duffy in 1880 that

> The chief skill he possessed was making wonderful likenesses with pen and ink, struck off without premeditation, and which it was found he could not afterwards inprove. Jane had some of these in letters from him, where the illustrations were produced apparently as spontaneously as the letter.

Typical of these is the sketch of Jules Janin (plate 3), which also shows the economy with which Thackeray achieved his effects. It is this same economy which, again and again throughout his career as an illustrator, makes Thackeray's small vignettes so effective—provided the engraver is able accurately to translate the ink line into the woodcut line without loss of spontaneity. Of the samples which I have collected here, *The Irish Sketch Book* provides two outstanding examples of this thumb-nail portraiture in the sporting attorney (plate 34) and the car-boy (plate 37). It is needless

to multiply examples, but one should not forget *Notes of a Journey from Cornhill to Grand Cairo*, with its delightful self-portrait (plate 54), nor, in *Vanity Fair*, such delicious miniatures as Jos Sedley in his buggy (plate 91) or Becky with her scuttle of coals (plate 115). In all these I would stress the quality of simplicity for, while it might be argued that Thackeray lacked the technical expertise to achieve his effects by elaborating his drawing, it is pertinent to retort that he had little need to do so since he could achieve equally striking effects with the utmost economy of means, as for example in his sketch of his daughters out walking with their grandparents (plate 6) and its woodcut counterpart from *The Roundabout Papers* (plate 197).

Thackeray possessed a natural simplicity of style, then, and only at the beginning and end of his career was he influenced into an unnatural elaboration—in the full-page woodcuts in *Lovel the Widower* and *Philip* in 1860 and 1861 in response to the challenge of 'high art', and in 1838 in the etchings for Douglas Jerrold's *Men of Character*, when, as with so many of his young contemporaries, Cruikshank was the ideal to be imitated. In Thackeray's defence, so far as the latter is concerned, it can be pleaded not only that he had admired Cruikshank's work since his schooldays but that he knew the artist personally and was both to contribute to his comic annuals and, in 1840, to write a notably appreciative study of his work for *The Westminster Review*. However, Thackeray was too shrewd a self-critic not to realize how far his etchings fell short of the master's in both technique and draughtsmanship and, indeed, how alien Cruikshank's was to his own style. Having recovered from his Cruikshankian aberration, his art was able to develop easily and naturally and he was fortunate that, in his maturity, those fellow-artists at *Punch* whose influence he received—Doyle, Henning and to a lesser degree Leech—were masters of the simple line.

Although, then, this development could have followed naturally, it was undoubtedly helped on its way by Daniel Maclise, principal artist on *Fraser's Magazine*, with which Thackeray was then so closely associated, and an old acquaintance whom Thackeray had encountered during his first literary and artistic forays in London some eight years earlier.

Maclise was a master of the direct uncluttered line, a style more congruous with Thackeray's own. Very possibly the clean lines of the etchings for *The Paris Sketch Book* (plates 19, 20, 25 and 26) may be due to this influence. Clearly there is a great deal of Maclise's style of portraiture, exemplified by the series of men of letters whom he depicted in *Fraser's*, in the cameo quality in the faces of Jos and Old Sedley (plates 88 and 97), for example, in *Vanity Fair*.

As *Vanity Fair* marks the high point of Thackeray's writing, so he gives of his best in the illustrations which he provided for the novel. I have already mentioned some of the woodcut vignettes and shall discuss the woodcut initials later, but there is a quality about his etchings which he never quite reached again. In *Pendennis* he is particularly happy in portraying a number of the lesser characters, seeming, as always, to be most at home with the disreputable Costigan (plate 162), or Altamont (plate 137), the humble Fanny (plate 156), honest Sam Huxter (plates 163, 165) or old Bowes (plate 155), while the feeling behind 'Poor Pen' (plate 139) surmounts the sentimentality of the subject. *The Virginians* contains a decorative collection of historically accurate costume pieces which only really come to life when that life is low, as with the bailiffs (plate 180) or the street urchins (plate 181). However, there is a quality about his etchings for *Vanity Fair* totally unexpected in the illustrator of *Yellowplush*, *Catherine* and even of *The Paris Sketch Book*, and only slightly foreshadowed in *Comic Tales and Sketches*. Not that Thackeray's etchings for *Vanity Fair* are uniformly good; 'Mr Joseph in a State of Excitement' (plate 89) harks back in its stiffness to *The Paris Sketch Book*. Yet there is fine draughtsmanship in such

etchings as 'Rebecca makes acquaintance with a live Baronet' (plate 94) or 'Becky in Lombard Street' (plate 109), while the splendidly louring 'Mr Osborne's Welcome to Amelia' (plate 96) and the genuinely pathetic 'Mr Sedley at the Coffee House' (plate 97) show that Thackeray was capable upon occasion of ranging beyond the satiric, the humorous and the burlesque.

For this is where his real talent as an illustrator lay. It was the expression of a gusto, of a zest which personal tragedy could not diminish, and of a keen sense of the ridiculous which did not spare the artist himself (for example, plates 1 and 3). It emerges in his very first book *Flore et Zéphyr*, in the *pas seul* itself and the *extreme désespoir* it expresses (plate 14) and in the beer, the brandy-and-water and the dresser combing Zéphyr's wig in the very earthy dressing-room (plate 16) in so sharp a contrast with the ethereal world of the ballet stage. The same acknowledgement of the sordid realities behind the tinsel can be seen in the woodcut vignette of Mr Dolphin upbraiding the chorus (plate 148); yet Thackeray loved the theatre in all its forms, and the pantomime in particular (for example, plates 117–19): the clown and the ogre are both recurrent motifs in his woodcut initials (for example, plate 196), and its burlesque elements corresponded with Thackeray's own boisterous humour. It is a pity that in *Comic Tales and Sketches* Thackeray's illustrations of 'The Tremendous Adventures of Major Gahagan' are chaste by comparison with the Munchausen exploits under Wellesley and Lake of their hero, Major Goliah O'Grady Gahagan, Honourable East India Company's Service, Commanding Battalion of Irregular Horse, Ahmednuggar. His Yellowplushes and Jeameses have their element of burlesque as well, but perhaps he is at his most typical when parodying Charles Lever or G. P. R. James in 'Punch's Prize Novelists' with illustrations (plates 77–9) deliberately and deflatingly in the style of comic cuts.

However, some of Thackeray's best work in this vein is to be found in his initial letters, both the smaller variety drawn for *Punch* and the larger designs which he supplied for his novels. They also reveal at times one of Thackeray's most endearing characteristics, his ability to laugh at himself, as when (plate 160) he depicts himself being assailed by the creatures of his own imagination. Often the initial letter sets the scene for the chapter which it opens by burlesquing the mood of what is to come; elsewhere (and this tendency is particularly noticeable in such later novels as *The Virginians*) the initial letter will be merely descriptive and serve as an additional vignette illustration; and finally, and more rarely, these initials are symbolic and prefigure the action of the chapter. Thus the initial letter to Chapter IV of *Vanity Fair* (plate 100) shows a young lady trying to catch a fish, just as the chapter describes the way in which Becky Sharp angled for a proposal of marriage from Jos Sedley.

Curiously enough for someone whose contemporaries likened him to Hogarth, or to a Hogarth manqué, very little of this symbolism enters the full-page etchings or woodcuts. While the illustrations which Phiz supplied for Dickens' novels are loaded with symbolism in the tradition of Hogarth, Thackeray's etchings are almost completely free of it. They are purely illustrative, and Thackeray seems content simply to try to depict the scene or incident without loading it with extra meanings. By and large he is successful and the real value of the Thackeray illustration is that it provides the right atmosphere for the period in which the novels are set—a nebulous era somewhere between the Congress of Vienna and the fall of the July Monarchy—and for their milieu, which, although it has its grandeurs, has also its more real miseries in the procession of shabby bucks, sharpers and disreputable drunks so lovingly and so sharply observed.

No study of Thackeray's graphic work can escape the conclusion that because it is so variable—occasionally brilliant, generally professional and competent, sometimes rank bad and amateur—and although it is,

as the writer's visualization of his characters, an integral part of his creative work, yet it cannot stand scrutiny at the same high level as Thackeray's writing. But simply to dismiss his graphic work because it does not reach this standard is to do both it and its creator a grave injustice—for how many book illustrators reach the same peak in their art which Thackeray attains as author of *Vanity Fair?* In fact, his illustrations have considerable merit if judged in terms of the graphic work of their genre and period. Here, I repeat, *Punch* provides the criterion but the work needs to be studied, not through isolated examples, but in the original volumes where it rubs shoulders with that of the other *Punch* artists. And it passes this test successfully, it meets the standards set by Doyle and Leech and their fellows and does not disgrace the company it keeps. Thackeray might be incapable of supplying the full-page political cartoons, but in his smaller sphere he more than held his own, and this, surely, is no small achievement for a man who came into the trade virtually untrained.

To understand the nature of this achievement we must return to those crucial years between 1833 and 1836, the years in which Thackeray's fortune vanished in the Bengal bank failures and in which he met and married Isabella Shawe. Had he managed to curb or cure his addiction to gambling, had he been able to preserve enough of his inheritance to ensure a reasonable competence or had he married a rich wife instead of a penniless girl, it seems very unlikely that we should have had the author of *Vanity Fair*. Mr Thackeray would very probably have dabbled in literature, but since the characteristic of his *alter ego*, Philip Firmin, is idleness and since he would have lacked the spur and the discipline applied by poverty, it is very unlikely that he would have been able to realize his latent literary genius. In fact, rather than dabble in writing, he would have been far more certain to have dabbled in painting, which rated much higher in his aesthetic scheme of things. As Thackeray himself put somewhat graphically to his friend Edward Fitzgerald in a letter of 7 October 1836:

> I am sorry to say that I like newspaper work very much . . . but poor picture-painting is altogether neglected; and for this neglect I can give you *no* better illustration, than to tell you that it seems like quitting a beautiful innocent wife (like Mrs T. for instance) to take up with a brazen whore . . .

In the event, he was to pass the rest of his life with the brazen whore of writing for newspapers, magazines and book publishers and, although the beautiful innocent wife of painting receded further and further every year and although Thackeray knew she was unattainable, it was long before he would honestly admit it. The idyll of the painter's life floats like a will-o-the-wisp through his letters—as, when on holiday in Switzerland with his daughters in the summer of 1851, he writes on 21 July to Mrs Brookfield:

> O Lord how much better it is than riding in the Park and going to dinner at 8 o'clock! I wonder whether a residence in this quiet would ennoble one's thoughts permanently? —and get them away from mean quarrels intrigues, pleasures? make me write good books—turn poet perhaps or painter . . .

If we are to believe Thackeray, he nurtured this splendid delusion until the momentous day in 1851 when he first looked into *Illustrations of Scripture by an Animal Painter*. Then, as he wrote much later to his mother on 1 January 1857,

> I think the idea of turning painter was knocked on the head at Glasgow where I was so confounded by Mrs Blackburne's prodigious genius and saw she had a talent so infinitely superior to my little one—and I thought I had best blow that poor little farthing candle out, and think of it no more . . .

But Thackeray was being disingenuous. In fact, he had buried his aspirations of be-coming a painter some twenty years before. Writing to Mrs Brookfield on 5 February 1849, when on a visit to Paris, he admits: 'I went to see my old haunts when I came to Paris thirteen years ago and made believe to be a painter—just after I was ruined and before I fell in love and took to marriage & writing.' Thackeray knew that the painter's life was all a bit of a pose, but it needed the sharp lesson of marriage and the need to support his young family to drive the truth home. Had Thackeray never had to work for a living, should we really have had any paintings worth looking at? We should still have had the delightful pen-sketches in his letters (but who would have preserved his correspondence or even thought it worth preserving?) and we should still have had the drawing-room talent of 'The Count's Adventures' and 'The Bandit's Revenge'.[22] But it would have remained a drawing-room talent incapable of producing the full range of his work as a professional illustrator. Adversity produced a writer of genius; it also produced a most competent book artist. The very excellence of his writing detracts from his achievement as the illustrator of his own books, yet, as his friend Dr John Brown observed, 'He had a genuine gift for drawing. The delicious Book of Snobs is poor without his own woodcuts.' And, although one might not be prepared wholly to accept Henry Kingsley's obituary tribute in *Macmillan's Magazine* of February 1864, what he has to say about Thackeray's illustrations to *Vanity Fair* might also be applied to the body of his book illustration:

> For the first time we found a novelist illustrating his own books well. At times nay very often, we could see that the great brain which guided the hand, in its eagerness to fix the image on paper, made that hand unsteady; that in seeking after the end also, there had been some impatient neglect of the means: in other words, that Thackeray sometimes drew incorrectly, but more often did not. But notwithstanding this, there are very few vignettes . . . which when once seen, can be forgotten.

1 ·Design for an equestrian statue of the artist

a great lot o' rabbuts - they were of no use those rabbuts, the 21st way
to march the next day . I saw the men walking about on the last day

taking leave of their sweethearts (who will
probably be consoled by the Gleshers) I
was carried off by my brother in law through
the rain to see a great sight - the Regimental
soup tureens and dish covers before they
were sent away. 'Feel _that_' says he, Williams
'just feel the weight of that ' I was called
upon twice to try the weight of that soup
dish and expressed the very highest grati-
fication at being admitted to that privilege . Poor simple young fellows

2   Soldier of the 21st Foot with his wife

last night that life was the greatest of pleasures to him, that every morning
when he woke he was thankful to be alive (this is very tolerably like him)
that he was always entirely
happy, and had never known

any such thing as blue
devils or repentance a
satiety . I had great fun
giving him authentic
accounts of London . I told him that to see the people boxing in
the streets was a constant source of amusement to us; that in

3   Jules Janin

(I've drawn it shockingly she thought I took the gold pen - but there
was my Coachwoman a very lovely pretty girl whose name was Ange
lina Henrion and who told me she was heiress of fifteen horses and
six carriages wh her Papa left. As we were driving to etiquer we
met one of the carriages and Angelina cried out voilà Papa - and I
thought Papa looked a little queer at seeing his daughter drive a gentleman
of forty. But she amused me with her artless prattle, and Papa did not
know that I was suffering, from something not at all unlike Cholera

4 The Pony Trap

Mr. James de la Pluche presents respectful Comps to Mrs. Elliot and I am very sorry that he cannot igsept your genteel and pralight invitation rot he is engaged as you will be gladd to hear to meat Miss Virginia Pottle: and afterwoods to go to a friendly Swoary where praps a reverend genth lady by name of Br—kf-ld may cumsoal me for his igstreme disapintment in not meeting neither Mrs. E nor Miss P

PS. Respectfl Comps to the young lady who sang like a Sting

PS. Genteel regards to Miss K.E.P.

· 5 Page of a Letter to Mrs Perry

6   The artist's daughters walking with their grandparents

J. j.

J. is a Judge – his Lordships in a fury
Most likely with the Gemmen of the Jury.

7   Letter J

M .m.

M. is a Med'cine nasty foul & black
May Eddy ne'er have cause such stuff to
take.

8   Letter M

Lady Arabella looked down at the little Lady Emmeline with a glance of unutterable affection.
'Is she not like me?' asked the lively but frivolous Countess.
Arabella thought with a sigh. How like the cherub is to her father!
Poor Arabella!

'The Heiress of Pimlico.
Vol. I.

The good old admiral now Earl of Fitzmarlinspike had 'braved the battle and the breeze' for many years on every sea.
He wore the collar and grand Cross of his own order and the French Orders & and came into the saloon shortly after ten o clock

The Heiress of Pimlico.

THE ORPHAN OF PIMLICO

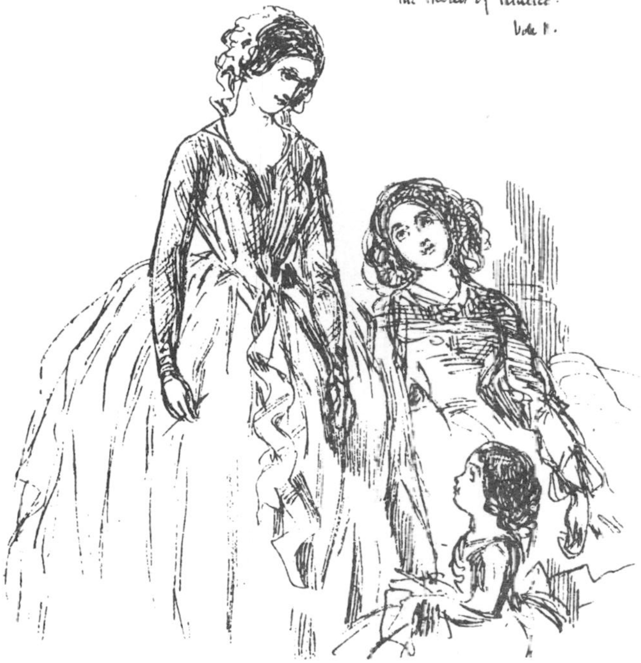

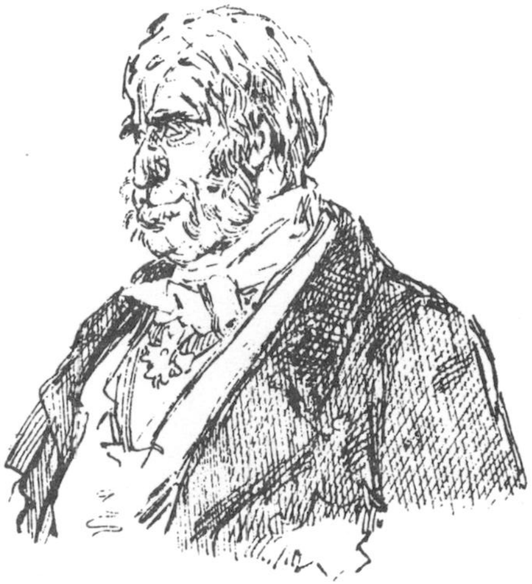

9 A page of text

10   The First Term (above); the Second Term (below)

11 King Louis Philippe

12 The actor Legier

13   *Flore déplore l'absence de Zéphyr*

14   *Dans un pas seul il exprime son extrême déspesoir*

15 *Réconciliation de Flore et Zéphyr*

16   *Les délassements de Zéphyr*

17 The Last Stroke of Fortune

18   Captain Brock appears at Court

19   Mr Pogson's Temptation

20 How to astonish the French

21   Hotel Touts

22   French Artist

23   The Gambler's Death (1)

24   The Gambler's Death (2)

25   French Catholicism

26   Rex, Ludovicus, Ludovicus Rex

27 Mrs Shum's Ejectment

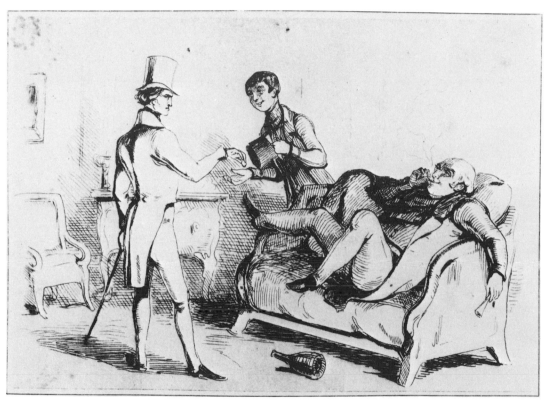

28   Mr Deuceace pays for his Papa's Cigars

29   The Major's Interview with a celebrated Character

30   Mr Adolphus Simcoe

"GIVE THAT CARD TO YOUR MASTER, AND SAY A GENTLEMAN WANTS TO SEE HIM."

31   Assumption of Aristocracy

32   The Landlord

33   The Nun

34   The Attorney

35   Galway

37   The Car-boy

36   The Trespasser

38   The Battle of Rheims

39   Nemours and Duke Jenkins

40 King Louis Philippe

41 Lord Brougham

THE LOWLY BARD TO HIS LADY LOVE.

(AIR—" *Oh, Nannie, wilt thou gang with me?*")

Oh lady, wilt thou wed with me,
　　And go and live at Camden Town ?
Can Hampstead Road have charms for thee ?
　　Canst thou to College Place come down ?

Say, wilt thou quit, without a sigh,
　　The bright *salons* of Belgrave Square ?
And canst thou, unrepining, fly
　　A two-pair-back with me to share ?

Oh wilt thou in the season, sweet,
　　Not sometimes weep for Rotten Row,
Where thou wast wont with TOM's *élite*
　　On summer afternoons to go ?

And oh, from round the corner, when
　　Our maid-of-all-work brings the beer,
Wilt thou not oft remember then
　　Thy footman, THOMAS, with a tear ?

When mem'ry paints the crimson plush,
　　And hat bedeck'd with golden braid,
Believ'st thou that thou wilt not blush
　　For slipshod JANE, our only maid ?

Britannia metal canst thou stand,
　　Off silver who was wont to dine ?
The vintage of a foreign land
　　Canst thou exchange for ginger wine ?

And tell me, canst thou sit and ply
　　Thy bodkin, love, my desk beside ?
Then, soon as I a ring can buy,
　　I 'll ask thee to become my bride.

———————

42　The Lowly Bard

PUNCH, 28 JUNE 1845

"WHY ARE YOU ON THE CROSSING, JAMES? IS YOUR FATHER HILL?"
"No. HE'S DROVE MOTHER DOWN TO HASCOT."

43   The Ascot Cup Day

PUNCH, 1 AUGUST 1846

"YOU SEEM IN LOW SPIRITS, JEM; YOU REALLY SHOULD GO INTO SOCIETY."

44   One "who can Administer to a Mind diseased"

"I'm in low sperits. A disagreeable insadent has just occurred. LADY PUMP, the banker's wife, asked me to dinner. I sat on her right, of coarse, with an uncommon gal ner me, with whom I was getting on in my fassanating way—full of lacy ally (as the Marquis says) and easy plesntry. Old PUMP, from the end of the table, asked me to drink Shampane; and on turning to tak the glass I saw CHARLES WACKLES (with womb I'd been imployed at COLONEL SPURRIERS' house) grinning over his shoulder at the Butler.

"The beest reckonized me. Has I was putting on my palto in the hall, he came up again: 'How dy doo, JEAMES,' says he, in a findish visper. 'Just come out here, CHAWLES,' says I, 'I've a word for you, my old boy.' So I beckoned him into Portland Place, with my pus in my hand, as if I was going to give him a sovaring.

"'I think you said "JEAMES," CHAWLES,' says I, 'and grind at me at dinner?'

"'Why, sir,' says he, 'we're old friends, you know.'

"'Take that for old friendship then,' says I, 'and I gave him just one on the noas, which sent him down on the pavemint as if he'd been shot.' And mounting myjesticly into my cabb, I left the rest of the grinning scoundrills to pick him up, & droav to the Clubb."

45   Charles Wrackles

wear it in her raving Air. I woar another in my butn-ole. Evns, what was my sattusfackshn as I leant hover her chair, and igsammined the house with my glas !

"She was as sulky and silent as pawsble, however—would scarcely speek ; although I kijoled her with a thowsnd little plesntries. I spose it was because that wulgar raskle SILVERTOP, *wood* stay in the box. As if he didn' know (Lady B's as deaf as a poast and counts for nothink) that people *sometimes* like a *tatytaty* "

46   Jeames at the Opera

ROYAL ACADEMY.

" DEAR PUNCH,   " *Newman Street, Tuesday.*

" ME and another chap who was at the Academy yesterday, agreed that there was *nothink in the whole Exhibition* that was worthy of the least notice—as our pictures wasn't admitted.

" So we followed about some of the gents., and thought we 'd *Exhibit the Exhibitors ;* among whom we remarked as follows. We remarked

MR. SNEAKER, R.A., particularly kind to MR. SMITH, a prize-holder of the Art-Union. N.B. SNEAKER always puts on a white Choaker on Opening day ; and has his boots *French pollisht.*

".Presently we examined MR. HOKEY, a-watching the effect of his picture upon a party who *looks* like a prize holder of the Art-Union. Remark the agitation in HOKEY'S eye, and the tremulous nervousness of his highlows. The old gent looks like a flat : but not such a flat as to buy HOKEY'S picture at no price. O no !

" Our eyes then turned upon that *seedy gent.,* ORLANDO FIGGS, who drew in our Academy for ten years.

Fancy FIGGS's delight at finding his picture on the line ! Shall I tell you how it got there ? *His aunt washes for an Academician.*

" The next chap we came to was

SEBASTIAN WINKLES, whose *profound disgust* at finding his portrait on the floor, you may *imadgin.* I don't think that queer fellow

PEOMBO RODGERS was much happier ; for his picture was hung on the ceiling. " But the most *riled* of all was

HANNIBAL FITCH, who found his picture wasn't received at all. Show 'em all up, dear *Mr. Punch,* and oblige your constant reader, " MODEST MERIT."

48   A Street view at Constantinople

49   Miriam

50   Lebanese Doll

51   The Horse-dealers

52   Negro Holiday in Alexandria

53   Zuleika   54   Self-portrait

55   Sydney Scraper

HERE is no disguising the fact that this series of papers is making a prodigious sensation among all classes in this Empire. Notes of admiration (!), of interrogation (?), of remonstrance, approval, or abuse, come pouring into *Mr. Punch's* box.   We have been called to task for betraying the secrets of three different families of DE MOGYNS; no less than four LADY SUSAN SCRAPERS have been discovered; and young gentlemen are quite shy of ordering half-a-pint of port and simpering over the *Quarterly Review* at the Club, lest they should be mistaken for SYDNEY SCRAPER, ESQ. "What *can* be your antipathy to Baker Street?" asks some fair remonstrant, evidently writing from that quarter.—"Why only attack the aristocratic Snobs?" says one estimable correspondent; "are not the snobbish Snobs to have their turn?"—"Pitch into the University Snobs!" writes an indignant gentleman, (who spells elegant with two l's.)—"Show up the Clerical Snob," suggests another. — "Being at MEURICE'S Hotel, Paris, some time since," some wag hints, "I saw LORD B., leaning out of the window with his boots in his hand, and bawling out, '*Garçon, cirez-moi ces bottes*' Oughtn't he to be brought in among the Snobs?"

56   Great City Snobs (initial)

57   "Oh, Mr. Snob! I'm afraid you're sadly satirical."

58   On Clerical Snobs (initial)

59   Dining-out Snobs (initial)

60 A Visit to some Country Snobs (initial) 61 On some Country Snobs (initial)

62 Mrs Ponto and Lady Hawbuck

63   Irish Peasant Couple

64   Mrs Gray and Polly

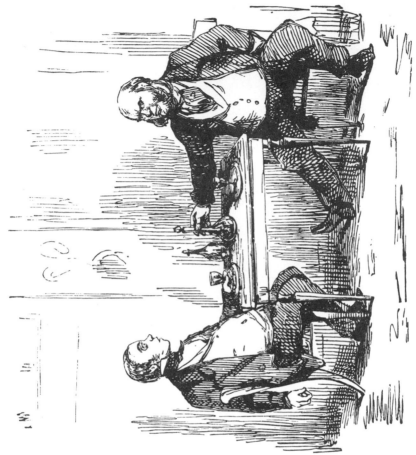

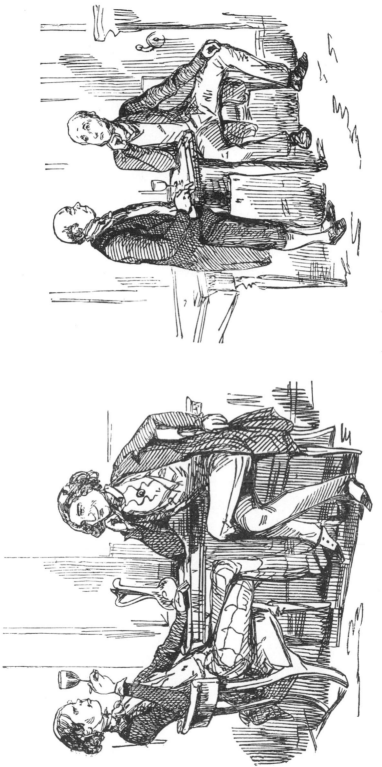

THE SNOBS OF ENGLAND (1846–7)
66 Club Snobs (2)

Kitchen Melodies.—Curry.

THREE pounds of veal my darling girl prepares,
And chops it nicely into little squares ;
Five onions next procures the little minx
(The biggest are the best, her SAMIWEL thinks),
And Epping butter nearly half-a-pound,
And stews them in a pan until they 're brown'd.

What 's next my dexterous little girl will do ?
She pops the meat into the savoury stew,
With curry-powder table-spoonfuls three,
And milk a pint, (the richest that may be)
And, when the dish has stewed for half-an hour,
A lemon's ready juice she'll o'er it pour :
Then, bless her ! then she gives the luscious pot
A very gentle boil—and serves quite hot.

P.S.—Beef, mutton, rabbit, if you wish ;
Lobsters, or prawns, or any kind of fish
Are fit to make A CURRY.   'Tis, when done,
A dish for Emperors to feed upon.

68   Title page

69   The Ball-room Door

70 Miss Bunnion

71 Miss Meggot

72 Cavalier Seul

73   George Grundsell

"I SAY, JIM, VICH DO YOU GIVE THE PRUFFERANCE? EUGENE SHUE OR
HALEXANDER DUMAS?"

74 Literature at a Stand

ancestral halls of the DE BARNWELLS, I felt that I was the NEMESIS
come to overthrow him. 'Dog,' I said to the trembling slave, 'tell me
where thy Gold is. *Thou* hast no use for it. I can spend it in relieving
the Poverty on which thou tramplest ; in aiding Science, which thou
knowest not ; in uplifting Art, to which thou art blind. Give Gold,
and thou art free ! ' But he spake not, and I slew him."

75   George de Barnwell

He was an old man—an old man evidently, too, of the Hebrew race —the light of his eyes was unfathomable—about his mouth there played an inscrutable smile. He had a cotton umbrella, and old trowsers, and old boots, and an old wig, curling at the top like a rotten old pear.

He sate down as if tired, in the first seat at hand, as RAFAEL made him the lowliest reverence.

"I am tired," says he; "I have come in fifteen hours. I am ill at Neuilly," he added with a grin. "Get me some *eau sucrée*, and tell me the news, PRINCE DE MENDOZA. These bread rows; this unpopularity of GUIZOT; this odious Spanish conspiracy against my darling MONTPENSIER and daughter; this ferocity of PALMERSTON against COLETTI, make me quite ill. Give me your opinion, my dear duke. But ha! whom have we here?"

Sir Raoul de Barbazure seized up the long ringlets of her raven hair. "Now!" shouted he to the executioner, with a stamp of his foot, "Now strike!"

The man (who knew his trade) advanced at once, and poised himself to deliver his blow: and, making his flashing sword sing in the air, with one irresistible, rapid stroke, it sheared clean off the head of

77   Barbazure (1)

the furious, the blood-thirsty, the implacable Baron de Barbazure!

Thus he fell a victim to his own jealousy; and the agitation of the Lady Fatima may be imagined, when the executioner, flinging off his mask, knelt gracefully at her feet, and revealed to her the well-known features of Romané de Clos Vougeot.

78   Barbazure (2)

But there was a movement among the enemy. An officer, glittering with orders, and another in a grey coat and a cocked hat, came to the wall, and I recognised the EMPEROR NAPOLEON and the famous JOACHIM MURAT.

"We are hardly pressed, methinks," NAPOLEON said, sternly. "I must exercise my old trade as an artillery-man;" and MURAT loaded, and the EMPEROR pointed the only hundred-and-twenty-four pounder that had not been silenced by our fire.

"Hurray, Killaloo boys!" shouted I. The next moment a sensation of numbness and death seized me, and I lay like a corpse upon the rampart.

79   Phil Fogarty

another glass of gin at his own expense, and they both drank it on the counter, where JOOLS talked of the affaers of Europ all night. To everything he said, the EARL OF YARDHAM answered " *Wee, wee ;*" except at the end of the evening, when he squeeged his & and said " *Bong swore.*"

"There 's nothing like goin amongst 'em to cquire the reel pronounciation," his Lordship said, as he let himself into his lodgings with his latch-key. " That was a very eloquent young gent at the Constantinople, and I 'll patronise him."

" *Ah, perfide, je te démasquerai !* " JOOLS remarked to himself as he went to bed in his Hotel de l'Ail. And they met the next night, and from that heavning the young men were continyonally together.

Well, one day, as they were walking in the Quadrant, JOOLS talking, and LORD YARDHAM saying " *Wee, wee,*" they were struck all of a heap by seeing—

But my paper is igshosted, and I must dixcribe what they sor in the nex number.

80 Crinoline

"OUR STREET."

BY

MR. M. A. TITMARSH.

LONDON:

CHAPMAN AND HALL, 186 STRAND.

MDCCCXLVIII.

81   Title page

82 Why our Nursemaids like Kensington Gardens

83   The Lady whom Nobody Knows

84   The Man in Possession

85 A Scene of Passion

86   The Note on the Pincushion

87   Rebecca's Farewell

88   Mr Joseph entangled

89   Mr Joseph in a state of excitement

90   The Misses Pinkerton

91   Mr Joseph's Buggy

92   Rebecca, Sir Pitt and Mrs Tinker

93   The Belgian Hussar

94   Rebecca makes acquaintance with a live Baronet

95 Miss Crawley's affectionate relatives

96   Mr Osborne's welcome to Amelia

97   Mr Sedley at the Coffee House

98   Mrs O'Dowd at the Flower Market

99   Venus preparing the armour of Mars

100   Chapter IV (initial)   101   Chapter XI (initial)

102   Chapter XXXIV (initial)

103   Chapter XXXVI (initial)

104   Chapter XXXVIII (initial)

105   Chapter XLIV (initial)

106   Chapter LX (initial)

107   Georgy makes aquaintance with a Waterloo Man

108   The Ribbons discovered in the fact

109   Becky in Lombard Street

110 Georgy goes to Church genteelly

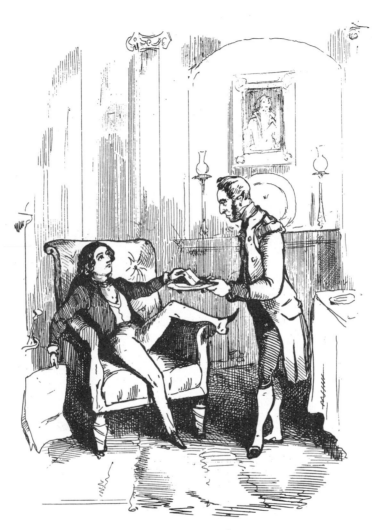

111 Georgy a Gentleman

112 A meeting

113   A fine Summer Evening

114 Jos performs a Polonaise

115   Becky and the coals

116   The Sharpers

E took possession of the private box assigned to us: and MRS. FLATHER seated herself in the place of honour —each of the young ladies taking it by turns to occupy the other corner. MISS MINNY and MASTER JONES occupied the middle places; and it was pleasant to watch the young gentleman throughout the performance of the comedy— during which he was never quiet for two minutes— now shifting his chair, now swinging to and fro upon it, now digging his elbows into the capacious sides of MRS. CAPTAIN FLATHER, now beating with his boots against the front of the box, or trampling upon the skirts of MRS. FLATHER's satin

117 A Night's Pleasure (initial)

118 Ballet Dancer

(which he was obliged to do pretty frequently, for he had taken cold while lying out among the rocks and morasses in the rainy miserable nights, so that the peasants, when they heard him snoring fitfully, thought that storms were abroad) at the gates of a castle by which he was passing, the door burst open, and the Irish Giant (afterwards Clown, indeed) came out, and wondering looked about, furious to see no one.

119   Pantomime Clown and Ogre

120   Young Mr Grigg

121   Old Mr Pogram

122 An invitation sent . . .

123 . . . and received

124   Truncheon

125   Initial O

126 Young Raphael

127   Rival Forces

128   The Caique

PUNCH, 17 MARCH 1849

OME time after the death of AURUNGZEBE, a mighty prince held domination over India, from the seven mouths of the Ganges to the five tails of the Indus, who was renowned above most other monarchs for his strength, riches, and wisdom. His name was KOOMPANEE JEHAN. Although this monarch had innumerable magnificent palaces at Delhi and Agra, at Benares, Boggleywollah, and Ahmednuggar, his common residence was in the beautiful island of Ingleez, in the midst of the capital of which, the famous city of Lundoon, KOOMPANEE JEHAN had a superb castle. It was called the Hall of Lead, and stood at the foot of the Mountain of Corn, close by the verdure-covered banks of the silvery Tameez, where the cypresses wave and the zendewans or nightingales love to sing. In this palace he sate and gave his orders, to govern the multitudinous tribes which paid him tribute from the Cashmerian hills to the plains watered by the Irrawaddy.

129   The Story of Koompanee Jehan (initial)

RESUMING that my dear BOBBY would scarcely consider himself to be an accomplished man about town, until he had obtained an entrance into a respectable Club; I am happy to inform you, that you are this day elected a Member of the Polyanthus, having been proposed by my kind friend, LORD VISCOUNT COLCHICUM, and seconded by your affectionate uncle. I have settled with MR. STIFF, the worthy Secretary, the preliminary pecuniary arrangements regarding the entrance fee and the first annual subscription—the ensuing payments I shall leave to my worthy nephew.

130   Initial letter P

F all the sciences which have made a progress in late years, I think, dear BOB (to return to the subject from which I parted with so much pleasure last week), that the art of dinner-giving has made the most delightful and rapid advances. Sir, I maintain, even now with a matured age and appetite, that the dinners of this present day are better than those we had in our youth, and I can't but be thankful at least once in every day for this decided improvement in our civilisation. Those who remember the usages of five-and-twenty years back will be ready, I am sure, to acknowledge this progress.—I was turning over at the Club yesterday a queer little book written at that period, which, I believe, had some authority at the time, and which records some of those customs which obtained, if not in good London Society, at least in some companies, and parts of our island. Sir, many of these practices seem as antiquated now, as the usages described in the accounts of Homeric feasts, or QUEEN ELIZABETH's banquets and breakfasts. Let us be happy to think they are gone.

131   Initial letter O

132   The Rosolio

133   Behind the Hay-ricks

134   Mr Roundhand looks out of the Window

135   The common Lot

136   The Judgment of Solomon

137   Colonel Altamont refuses to move on

138   The Curate come to Grief

139   Poor Pen

140   Chapter XII (initial)

141   Chapter XIII (initial)

142   Chapter XVII (initial)

143   Chapter XXVI (initial)

144   Chapter XXXVI (initial)

145   Pen's Staircase—I

146   Pen's Staircase—2

147   Sir Derby Oaks

148   Mr Dolphin

149   Mr Bludyer

150   Captain Costigan

151   Mirobolant fascinates the natives

152　An Escape

153   Almost perfect Happiness

154   The Costigan at the Porter's Lodge

155   On the look out

156 Pen's Nurse

157　At the Spa

158　The Chevalier Strong

159   Chapter L (initial)

160   Chapter LI (initial)

161   Chapter LV (initial)

162   The Captain won't go home till morning

163   Mr Samuel asks a question

164   Mr Morgan at his ease

165   Mr Huxter asks pardon

166   The German Peasant Maiden

167   "Schlafen sie wohl"

168   King Valoroso

169   His Queen

170   The Countess Gruffanuff

171 Betsinda

172   The Rivals

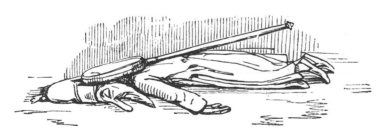

173   Prince Giglio and the Warming-pan

174   The Execution Warrant

175   Angelica arrives just in Time

176 Count Hogginarmo

in the morning, fancying himself in the Royal Palace at home, called, " John, Charles, Thomas ! My chocolate—my dressing-gown—my slippers ;" but nobody came. There was no bell, so he went and bawled out for waiter on the top of the stairs.

The landlady came up, looking—looking like this—

" What are you a hollaring and a bellaring for here, young man ? " says she.

" There's no warm water—no servants ; my boots are not even cleaned."

" He, he ! Clean 'em yourself," says the landlady. " You young students give yourselves pretty airs. I never heard such impudence."

" I'll quit the house this instant," says Giglio.

" The sooner the better, young man. Pay your bill and be off. All my rooms is wanted for gentlefolks, and not for such as you."

" You may well keep the Bear Inn," said Giglio. " You should have yourself painted as the sign."

The landady of the Bear went away *growling*. And Giglio returned to his room, where the first thing he saw was the fairy

177   The Landlady

178   Prince Bulbo in Prison

179 Gather ye Rosebuds while ye may

180   A pair of old Acquaintances

181 George's Friends

182   Chapter IX (initial)

183   Chapter LII (initial)

184   Chapter LXIV (initial)

185   Chapter LXVI (initial)

186   Chapter LXXI (initial)

187   Chapter LXXXVIII (initial)

188   Arbitrium popularis auræ

189 Bessy's Spectacles

190   Chapter II (initial)

191   Chapter III (initial)

192   Chapter I (initial)

193   Chapter VI (initial)

194   On Some Late Great Victories (initial)

195   Round About the Christmas Tree (initial)

196   Ogres (initial)

197   Notes of a Week's Holiday (initial)

198   A lazy idle Boy (initial)

Notes to the Introduction

1 Sketches from it are reproduced in John Camdem Hotten's *Piccadilly Annual* (1870).

2 A number of the plates which he etched at Cambridge survived and later passed into the hands of the antiquarian bookseller Sotheran, who rather unfairly issued these immature efforts in 1878 as *Etchings by the late William Makepeace Thackeray*.

3 Professor Gordon N. Ray has estimated his losses at the tables as about £3000.

4 'I have made a wood-cut [for *The National Standard*] of Louis-Philippe wh: is pretty good,' Thackeray wrote to his mother on 2 May 1833. We may not share his enthusiasm for the result (plate 11); he was to do better with this cartoonists' favourite later (for example, plates 40, 76). Given Thackeray's gaming habits, it is interesting to note that among the woodcuts which he designed for *The National Standard* was one of 'Mr Crockford' (3 August 1833).

5 Major Frederick Goldsmith, in 'Reminiscences of Thackeray' (*Athenaeum*, May 1891), suggests that Thackeray produced a number of caricatures and sketches for the print-sellers, specifying a portrait of 'the African Roscius', the negro actor Ida Aldridge. To this class belong a cartoon for *The Anti-Corn–Law Review* (1839) and a rather feeble imitation of Cruikshank, the satiric print 'Britannia protecting the Drama', of the same period.

6 Henry Van Duzer's *A Thackery Library* credits him with the illustrations to C. G. Addison's travel-book, *Damascus and Palmyra*, and in addition he drew the designs for two little books, the anonymous *King Glumpus* (1837) and John Barrow's *The Exquisites* (1839). He abandoned his illustrations to 'The Ballad of Lord Bateman' when he heard that Cruikshank was thinking of illustrating it (1839).

7 Although at first sight it seems as if eight years of strenuous activity had increased his literary page-rate by only two-thirds, whereas his artistic rate had tripled, it is deceptive. He was quoting Fraser the price of a *drawing* (which somebody else would have to etch or transfer to the lithographic stone), while for *Vanity Fair* he quotes the price of an *etched plate*. The rise is not therefore so dramatic as it might appear. Thackeray seems to have been charging the then going rate, since at about this time Phiz was charging much the same price, and he was at the top of his profession. Thackeray's fee, however, did include the woodcut initials and vignettes.

8 Hence the over-intense friendship with Mrs Brookfield and the more than mere flirtation with Sally Baxter on his first American tour. Nor was it less symptomatic of his wry view of his own matrimonial frustrations that the narrator in *Doctor Birch*, *The Kickleburys* and *Lovel the Widower*, for example, is equally the victim of frustrated passion. Thackeray was clearly a sensual man who compensated for his deprivations in these friendships and in a gluttonous enjoyment of food and drink.

9 It was, however, published by Macrone. Chapman & Hall issued *The Irish Sketch*

Book and the Christmas books; Bradbury & Evans (publishers of *Punch*), *Vanity Fair* and the novels written before Thackeray became associated with George Smith's *Cornhill Magazine;* and Smith's company, Smith, Elder, the later novels and the posthumous collected works.

10 The books were issued either 'plain' or 'coloured'. In fact the 'plain' copies have a border and a yellow tint printed over the woodcuts, this second colour being very cleverly used to heighten their effect. The illustrations selected from *Our Street* (plates 81–5) and from *The Kickleburys on the Rhine* (plates 166–7) are reproduced from 'plain' copies; those from *Mrs Perkins's Ball* (68–73) from woodcuts before the addition either of colour or of a yellow tint.

11 For example, Thackeray sent his publishers, Chapman & Hall, a specimen of the Parisian children's broadsheet on 19 January 1843, suggesting that he supply a substitute English text and that they print the pictures from electrotypes of the French blocks. In the event nothing transpired, but interestingly enough, some five years later in a precisely similar sort of transaction, Chapman & Hall became the publishers of the English editions of Hetzel's delightful series of illustrated books for children, *Le nouveau magasin des enfants.*

12 This made for its continued popularity and it was reissued in 1860 and 1865 by two different publishers. It is a reflexion of the sentimental taste of the 1860s that both the new publishers should drop two macabre but highly effective woodcuts typical of the earlier but more robust romantic style.

13 Louis Marvy (1815–50) was a French engraver whom Thackeray first met in Paris in 1841 and with whom he was on very close terms. When Marvy was forced to seek temporary political asylum in England in 1848, Thackeray assisted him by writing the text and finding a publisher for the series of etchings reproduced by his special colour process—*Sketches after the English Landscape Painters.* Marvy returned to France in 1849, but his early death left his widow destitute and Thackeray for many years supported Madame Marvy financially.

14 When in 1850 *The Examiner* and *The Morning Chronicle*, irritated by the realistic and satiric portrait of the literary underworld which Thackeray paints in *Pendennis*, 'offered (him) up to general reprehension in two leading articles . . .: by the latter for "fostering a baneful prejudice" against literary men; by the former, for "stooping to flatter" this prejudice in the public mind, and "condescending to caricature (as is too often my habit) my literary fellow-labourers, in order to pay court to "the non-literary class"', he was moved to write to the editor of *The Morning Chronicle* in protest. In his long letter (from which I have already quoted), he firmly rebuts these charges, makes it plain that he has no quarrel with the status accorded to writers in Victorian England, regards literature as a profession like any other and insists 'that it is the duty of the literary man, as well as any other, to practise regularity and sobriety, to love his family and pay his tradesmen'. The pretentious, the dishonest and the immoral were as fit targets for satire as their counterparts in any other profession. Since he himself subscribed to the highest professional standards, Thackeray was particularly upset by an article in *Le revue des deux mondes* of September 1854 in which Paul Emile Forgues suggested that in his lectures he 'had praised Addison in order to curry favour with the English aristocracy'. In his letter of protest to Forgues he retorted: 'I have been earning my own bread with my pen for near twenty years now; and sometimes very hardly too, but in the worst time, please God, never lost my own respect.'

15 Richard Doyle, as a Roman Catholic,

had been driven to resign from *Punch* in 1851 by the magazine's rabidly anti-Catholic attitude to 'Papal Aggression'—the restoration of the English Catholic hierarchy. Although Thackeray himself was staunchly Protestant, he supported Doyle as a friend for whom he had the warmest feelings. His appreciation of Doyle's talents as an artist may be found in his commissioning him to illustrate his books, in the influence which Doyle undoubtedly exercised upon Thackeray and in the glowing tribute which he paid in *The Morning Chronicle* (26 December 1845) to Doyle as illustrator of *The Fairy Ring*, J. E. Taylor's translation of a selection of Grimm's fairy stories.

16 Although his *English Humourists* and *Four Georges* are light-weight lecture material, he had gained through his researches for *Esmond* a profound knowledge of the early eighteenth century, and considered seriously at one time continuing Macaulay's *History of England*.

17 Did Thackeray remember this review when he excused himself for costuming the characters in *Vanity Fair* in the style of the 1840s rather than that of their time by pleading the ugliness of Regency dress?

18 Evidence for the account given here comes from George Smith's own recollections as given in Huxley's *House of Smith, Elder*, backed by supporting letters from Thackeray to Walker. There is, however, so strong a family likeness between the plates in *Philip* which Walker is known to have 'improved' and the illustrations in *Lovel the Widower* as makes it not unreasonable to suspect his assistance from the very start of Thackeray's association with George Smith and *The Cornhill Magazine*. This assistance must also have extended to some at least of the initial letters in these two novels—Sir Edwin Landseer supplied the drawing of the black sheep for Chapter IV of his

friend's *Lovel the Widower*—and indeed to those of *The Roundabout Papers* as well: contrast the pure Thackeray of plates 193, 196 and 197 with the other initials (plates 190, 191, 194 and, especially, 192 and 195).

19 Leech entered Charterhouse when Thackeray was already a senior boy, but he remembered him when they met again as colleagues on *Punch*. They became very close personal friends and the novelist stood godfather to one of the artist's sons. By praising Leech in this essay as the mainstay of *Punch*, Thackeray caused considerable offence to his erstwhile colleagues on the magazine.

20 An extreme example of this criticism, roused by something so apparently innocuous as *The Newcomes*, appeared in the January 1856 issue of the Boston *Christian Examiner*, when the reviewer wrote: 'Through the fresh delineation [in novels] of early life, devoted affection, local, traditional, and social charms, the dormant fatih in humanity and obscured perspectives of time are renewed to the vision and the heart. In the hands of genial artists . . . this moral refreshment is sure to be imparted . . . Now the radical objection to Mr Thackeray's pictures of life is, that they are utterly devoid of seriousness. . . . It is, however, in the female character that Mr Thackeray's want of refined perception and elevated sentiment emphatically betrays itself. No modern writer has done more to strip from the very name of woman all associations of moral beauty. It is not merely that he embodies the deceit, meanness, indelicacy, and selfish hardihood possible to the sex,—that he exhibits female monsters, approaches to which unfortunately exist and are fair subjects for the gallery of a novelist who professes to deal with realities; but it is that these revolting types of perverted womanhood, or rather unsexed human deformities, are not redeemed in

his pages by characters of equal force and finish of the opposite qualities. . . . One would imagine that it had never been Mr Thackeray's privilege really to know, intimately to appreciate, and absolutely to recognize, a truly noble, gifted lovely woman. Otherwise a celestial grace would have been unconsciously woven into his "dream of fair women" . . .'

21 I have already cited a number of instances of this faculty, especially in connexion with his etching and painting endeavours in Paris in the 1830s. Later, during his Irish tour, he wrote to his mother on 1 September 1842 confessing, 'I have made as regards drawing half a dozen abominable attempts at landscapes, than wh: many a child could do better; and shall confine the drawings for the book to figures almost entirely. How strange this is, I mean the bad landscape drawing, in a person with an exceedingly strong perception of natural beauty.' And right at the close of his career he could admit to her in a letter of 5 July 1862 that, 'Yesterday I spent all day . . . making a very bad drawing. Young Walker who is twenty does twice as well.'

But, if aware of his own weaknesses, he must equally have known where his talents lay, as he shows, perhaps quite unconsciously, in a very self-revealing criticism of Phiz's illustrations to Charles Lever's *Our Mess*, which 'shew to great advantage the merits of that dashing designer. He draws a horse admirably, a landscape beautifully, a female figure with extreme grace and tenderness; but as for its humour, it is stark naught; nay, worse, the humorous faces are bad caricatures, without, as I fancy, the slightest provocation to laughter. If one were to meet these monsters expanded from two inches to six feet, people would be frightened by them, not amused, so cruel are their grimaces and unearthly their ugliness.' For, whether he was aware of it or not, Thackeray praises Phiz for his achievements in those areas of drawing in which the critic himself was manifestly incapable (or less capable) and attacks him for his work in precisely that department in which, even by February 1844 (the date of this review in *Fraser's*), Thackeray was making or hoped himself to make a mark, namely, caricature and burlesque.

22 'The Count's Adventures' is an extravaganza based on the imaginary adventures in Spain of Thackeray's friend of his early days in Paris, the Scots artist John Grant Brine. It is reproduced in *The Letters and Private Papers of W. M. Thackeray* (Vol I, Appendix V, pp 509 ff), edited by Gordon N. Ray, from the original manuscript in the Widener Collection at Harvard University. 'The Bandit's Revenge' is a delightful spoof on the production of a new tragedy by a provincial theatrical company, complete with the reviews in the rival local newspapers. The original manuscript is preserved in the Department of Prints and Drawings, British Museum, where it is bound into the same volume as 'Simple Melodies'.

Volume Publication of Thackeray's
Early Writings

The publishing history of Thackeray's early writings offers ample evidence to show how slow was the growth and how modest the extent of the reputation which the novelist enjoyed with the wider reading public until the publication of *Vanity Fair* in parts between January 1847 and July 1848 thrust him to the forefront.

Flore et Zéphyr is satiric art rather than literature and Thackeray's first real books, *The Paris Sketch Book* (1840) and *Comic Tales and Sketches* (1841), are collections of articles and stories written originally for the magazines. Both were printed in editions of around 500 copies and neither sold particularly well. Better success attended *The Irish Sketch Book:* its first print in 1843 was larger and it went into a second edition in 1845. By these standards *Notes of a Journey from Cornhill to Grand Cairo* was a major success with two editions in 1846, the year of publication; yet it was more probably Thackeray's reputation as a contributor to *Punch* (his 'Snobs of England' had begun to appear at the end of February 1846) which inspired Chapman & Hall to publish, and to publish successfully, the first of his Christmas books, *Mrs. Perkins's Ball*, in December of that year.

'The Snobs of England' achieved separate volume publication with the original illustrations as *The Book of Snobs* in 1848, but the bulk of Thackeray's early writing (and this included such masterly novels as *Barry Lyndon* and *A Shabby Genteel Story*) were not re-issued until 1855-7 in what effectively constitutes their first British editions. Not until

Thackeray's fame as a novelist was secure did Bradbury & Evans reprint his early fictions, published simultaneously in four collected volumes of *Miscellanies* and as separate works. None of the volumes is illustrated and their content is as follows:

VOLUME I (1855)
Ballads
The first collection of Thackeray's occasional verse.

The Book of Snobs
A reprint of the 1848 edition. It omitted the original Chapters XVII-XXIII, which Thackeray considered 'so stupid, so personal, so snobbish' that he suppressed them.

The Tremendous Adventures of Major Gahagan
Reprinted from Volume II of *Comic Tales and Sketches*

The Fatal Boots and *Cox's Diary*
These had provided the main text for George Cruikshank's *Comic Almanacks* of 1839 and 1840 respectively. The former is also known as 'Stubbs's Calendar'. The two pieces were printed together in the separate volume issue.

VOLUME II (1856)
The Memoirs of Mr. Charles J. Yellowplush
A reprint of Volume I of *Comic Tales and Sketches*.

The Diary of C. Jeames de la Pluche Esq.
Reprints of the *Punch* material of 1845-6

and combined with the preceding item as a separate volume.

Sketches and Travels in London
A reprint of the *Punch* articles of 1847-8, including 'Mr. Brown's Letters to a Young Man about Town' of 1848-9.

Novels by Eminent Hands
A reprint of 'Punch's Prize Novelists'.

Character Sketches
A reprint of the text matter which Thackeray had contributed to Kenny Meadows' *Heads of the People* (1840-1). Combined with the preceding item as a separate volume.

VOLUME III (1856)
The Memoirs of Barry Lyndon
Reprinted with corrections from *Fraser's Magazine* (1844). Thackeray never illustrated this novel.

The Legend of the Rhine
A reprint of the story which Thackeray had originally contributed to *George Cruikshank's Table Book* (June-December 1845).

Rebecca and Rowena
A reprint of the Christmas book of 1849-50. Included with the preceding item in separate volume publication. Neither, of course, had Cruikshank's or Doyle's original illustrations.

A Little Dinner at Timmins's
A reprint of the *Punch* articles (1848).

The Bedford Row Conspiracy
Reprinted from Volume II of *Comic Tales and Sketches*. Combined with the preceding item as a separate volume.

VOLUME IV (1857)
The Fitzboodle Papers and *Men's Wives*
A reprint of the material from *Fraser's Magazine* (1842-3). Combined as a separate volume.

A Shabby Genteel Story
Reprinted from *Fraser's Magazine* (1840).

The History of Samuel Titmarsh and the Great Hoggarty Diamond
First appeared in *Fraser's Magazine* (1841) when, like the preceding items, it had not been illustrated. Thackeray issued a separate edition with his revisions and illustrations in 1849.

A very similar situation obtained in the United States of America. Although the absence of any copyright protection allowed American publishers to pirate British authors at will, Thackeray's reputation in the early days was never such as to invite this practice. Thus, and with some curious exceptions, it was his fame as the author of *Vanity Fair* and his popularity as a lecturer which induced the New York house of D. Appleton & Co to issue a number of his early writings between 1852 and 1853, and in this way to make their American editions Thackeray 'firsts'. The books concerned were these:

1852   *The Confessions of Fitzboodle*
        (with *The Tremendous Adventures
        of Major Gahagan*)
        Men's Wives
        A Shabby Genteel Story (with 'The
        Professor', 'The Bedford Row
        Conspiracy' and 'A Little Dinner
        at Timmins's)
        The Yellowplush Papers

1853   *Barry Lyndon* (in the original version
        as it appeared in *Fraser's*)
        Jeames's Diary (with *A Legend of the
        Rhine* and *Rebecca and Rowena*)
        Mr. Brown's Letters (for which
        Thackeray wrote a preface, dated
        New York, December 1852)
        The Paris Sketch Book
        Punch's Prize Novelists (with 'Travel
        Notes of a Fat Contributor'—
        Punch 1844-5—and 'Travels in
        London')

As with the Bradbury & Evans reprints, these volumes are not illustrated.

Of his other early writings, J. Winchester of New York had published *The Irish Sketch Book* (with Thackeray's illustrations) in 1843, the year of the first Chapman & Hall edition, and in 1848 Harper Brothers rushed out an unillustrated edition of *The Great Hoggarty Diamond*, reprinted direct from *Fraser's*, ahead of the revised and illustrated English edition. Meanwhile S. N. Dickinson of Boston took 'Stubbs's Calendar' for their *People's Almanac* of 1842, reproducing Cruikshank's illustrations. Perhaps they printed additional plates in anticipation of a non-existent demand, for when in 1850 Stringer & Townsend of New York published *Stubbs's Calendar* they issued it with less than the original twelve plates. Moreover, Van Duzer shows that the plates themselves vary from copy to copy, one which he examined having numbers 1, 3, 5, 7, 9, 11 and 12, another 2, 4, 6, 8, 10 and 11.

However, C. J. Yellowplush is the one Thackeray character to achieve really early publication in the United States, *The Diary of Jeames C. de la Pluche* being published by William Taylor of New York in 1846, after the series ended in *Punch* in January of that year, and with Thackeray's original illustrations reproduced. However, it is to the American publishers of *The Yellowplush Correspondence*, E. L. Carey & A. Hare of Philadelphia, that the signal honour belongs not simply of anticipating a British volume publication of the work, but, by issuing their edition in 1839, of making it Thackeray's first published prose work in volume form.

List of Illustrations

188

Index